Innovative
Approaches to
Counseling

RESOURCES FOR
CHRISTIAN COUNSELING

RESOURCES FOR CHRISTIAN COUNSELING

Volume One
Innovative Approaches to Counseling   *Gary R. Collins*

Volume Two
Counseling Christian Workers   *Louis McBurney*

Volume Three
Self-Talk, Imagery, and Prayer in Counseling   *H. Norman Wright*

Volume Four
Counseling Those With Eating Disorders   *Raymond E. Vath*

(Other volumes forthcoming.)

Innovative Approaches to Counseling

GARY R. COLLINS, Ph.D.

RESOURCES FOR
CHRISTIAN COUNSELING

General Editor

Gary R. Collins, Ph.D.

WORD BOOKS
PUBLISHER
WACO, TEXAS
A DIVISION OF
WORD, INCORPORATED

Library of Congress Cataloging-in-Publication Data

Collins, Gary R.
  Innovative approaches to counseling.

  (Resources for Christian counseling; v. 1)
  Bibliography: p.
  Includes index.
  1. Pastoral counseling. 2. Counseling. I. Title.
II. Series.
BV4012.2.C565 1986   253.5   86–11065
ISBN 0–8499–0510–9

6 7 8 9 8 FG 9 8 7 6 5 4 3 2 1
Printed in the United States of America

CONTENTS

FOREWORD

AS EVERY COUNSELOR is well aware, we currently are living in the midst of a "counseling boom." Surely there has never been a time in history when so many people are aware of psychological issues, concerned about personal problems, interested in psychological writings, and willing to talk about their insecurities, inadequacies, and intimate concerns. Within only a few decades we have seen the birth of a great host of theories, degree programs, books, seminars, articles, new journals, radio programs, films, and tape presentations that deal with counseling. Numerous counselors have appeared— some with good training and great competence, but others with little sensitivity and not much awareness of what they are trying to accomplish.

Perhaps it is not surprising that the counseling field is confusing to many people, threatening to some, and often criticized both within the church and without. Nevertheless, people still struggle with psychological and spiritual problems, stress is both a personal and social issue, and many seek help from counselors.

And how does the counselor keep abreast of latest developments? Many turn to books, but it is difficult to know which of the many volumes on the market are of good quality and which are not. The Resources for Christian Counseling series is an attempt to provide books that give clearly written, practical, up-to-date overviews of the issues faced by contemporary Christian counselors. Written by counseling experts, each of whom has a strong Christian commitment, the books are intended to be examples of accurate psychology and careful use of Scripture. Each will have a clear evangelical perspective, careful documentation, a strong practical orientation, and freedom from the sweeping statements and undocumented rhetoric that sometimes characterize books in the counseling field.

The Resources for Christian Counseling books will together comprise a complete encyclopedia of Christian counseling. As General Editor, I am honored to have this volume launch a series that could significantly influence the lives of many people. And I am enthusiastic about those who have agreed to write the volumes that follow. All of us hope that these books will be useful, practical, accurate guides for those who are privileged and challenged to be effective Christian counselors.

Gary R. Collins, Ph.D.
Kildeer, Illinois

INTRODUCTION

IT BOTHERED ME when I first realized that I didn't like counseling.

I was steeped in a competitive and challenging doctoral program in clinical psychology. All of my classmates were enthusiastic about their courses, practicums, and early experiences as emerging professional counselors. We read what must have been hundreds of books and journal articles, wrote papers, met with clients, interacted with professors, and discussed our work over endless cups of coffee in the student union. I discovered—for the first time—that I could be a good student. The classes and discussions were stimulating, and there was plenty of evidence that my counseling was effective. People were getting better.

But counseling bored me.

Things were no more interesting after I got my degree and accepted a position in the counseling center of a local state university. I had—and still have—an intense interest in "people-helping." But surely there could be other ways to help besides sitting in a room discussing problems on a one-to-one basis. Weren't a lot of people being helped by their families and churches, even without professional psychotherapy? Didn't many find help by reading books or talking things over with a neighbor? Couldn't many be helped to work on their own problems and sometimes to avoid problems before they arose? Was it true that a lot of good counseling is done in church foyers, cars, restaurants, hospital rooms, airplanes, or even on street corners? Was the student correct who stated that I was a good "sidewalk counselor" who frequently talked over problems with students while we walked to class?

In those early days, such questions forced me to struggle with my professional identity. How could I be a licensed clinical psychologist, a teacher of counseling, and, later, a writer of counseling books when I was bored in the counseling room? Slowly, I began to realize that people-helping is like a diamond with many sides. Working with people in the privacy and confidentiality of a counseling office is of crucial importance, but often there are other, less traditional approaches to counseling that can be of equal and sometimes even greater effectiveness.

This book describes some of these approaches. They have been used, often informally, for many years, but they nevertheless are considered "nontraditional" and "innovative" because they only recently have come to be accepted as important and powerful instruments in the people-helper's toolbox of resources. In my own work, these are the approaches that get used most often—and, for me, they work best.

In writing about these approaches, I am again reminded of three issues that are of constant concern whenever I produce something for publication.

First, I want to strive for quality. For me, that means a clear, concise, well-organized writing style; the highest possible accuracy in both the text and documentation; carefully thought-out conclusions; an awareness of the cultural implications of what is being written; content that is interesting and "fun to read" even when it is intended primarily to be informative; and an avoidance of "cute clichés" or case histories that may decorate a book but contribute nothing of real value. Quality writing involves the careful use of Scripture and an unbiased reporting of psychological conclusions. Writers usually fall short of such lofty aspirations, but my goal is to keep working to produce writing that is accurate, informative, clear, and interesting.

Second, I strive to avoid repetition. One of my friends is the author of over fifteen books, but they all seem to say the same thing in slightly different ways. When you've read one or two of his books, you have the message that permeates them all. My friend probably doesn't see this duplication (authors tend to be blind to their own weaknesses). He would agree that continual repetition is unfair to bookbuyers and to readers who may have limited resources and time for reading.

The book in your hands deals with some themes that have been considered in my earlier writings (pastoral counseling, laypeople-helping, self-help, and prevention of problems, to name a few), and I am well aware of the possibility for repetition. To avoid this, I have gone over the following pages carefully and compared them with my previous books. Some of my colleagues have done the same. I have tried to produce a book that is a fresh new approach to people-helping—a volume that goes beyond what has been written before.

Third, this book is intended to be practical, clearly stating what will work and "how to do it." Practical writing surely must also be precise, must avoid simplistic formulas, and should give evidence to indicate why the author's suggestions can be expected to work.

As with most of my books, this one has been in the planning stage for several years before anything was put on paper. Some of these ideas began to form in my mind when I was still in graduate school. My thinking was greatly stimulated when I discovered the field of "community psychology" with its growing literature. I have been challenged by students in the several community psychology and pastoral psychology classes that have been taught over the past few years at Trinity Evangelical Divinity School. On a number of occasions, both at home and overseas, at pastors' conferences and seminary lectureships, I have given lectures on nontraditional approaches to counseling. The preparation for, delivery of, and reaction to these talks have helped to refine much of my thinking.

Helpful, too, have been my discussions with Ernie Owen and his colleagues at Word, Inc., and my interactions with eminent Christian counselors, whose keen, perceptive insights will be available through the Resources for Christian Counseling book series, which I am honored to edit. To all of these people, and to others who have helped in quiet ways, I am deeply grateful for their input, suggestions, observations, and encouragement. My name may be on the cover, but this book clearly involves the ideas of a multitude of insightful people.

Once again, the chief of these insightful supporters has been my wife, Julie. More than any others, she and our daughters, Marilynn and Jan, continue to make my writing possible. I never want to forget their encouragement, and neither do I want to slip into the incredible position of ignoring my family and their needs so I can write books about caring and people-helping.

The apostle Paul once described his life work in a few concise words: to proclaim Christ "admonishing and teaching" everyone with all wisdom so that he might present everyone complete in Christ. For this purpose, Paul wrote, "I labor, striving according to His power, which mightily works within me" (Col. 1:28, 29, NAS). This is a magnificent example for us all—to work, empowered by Christ, with the intention of helping others to become complete in Christ. It is my prayer that this book will help us all to reach more effectively toward that goal.

Innovative
Approaches to
Counseling

RESOURCES FOR
CHRISTIAN COUNSELING

CHAPTER ONE

COMMUNITY COUNSELING

IS IT EVER QUIET in Vellore? When I think of that fascinating city, my mind fills with images of people—in cars, on bicycles, crowded on sidewalks and spilling over into the roads, sitting on the curbs, begging near the church, hawking their wares in the markets, visiting with friends in the streets, riding in crawling oxcarts. All seem oblivious to the darting motorbikes, the weaving taxis, the noisy buses, and the emaciated cows that wander nonchalantly through the streets of India, undisturbed and seemingly unaware of the ever-present swarms of humanity.

Only the coldest, most self-centered visitor could observe this scene and fail to be moved by the smells, sounds, and sights of India. There are modern buildings, comfortable houses, and gracious people—many of whom have welcomed me into their homes. But it is impossible to miss the indescribable poverty and the dusty, rickety shacks where so many spend their lives without electricity, plumbing, or furniture. It is deeply sobering to ponder the needs of those people and to see the signs of superstition and spiritual darkness.

Could it be in Vellore that some of the most innovative approaches to counseling have been developed? Assisted by a small but hard-working and dedicated staff, Dr. B. J. Prashantham has seen his Christian counseling center grow beyond its original church sponsorship. Its influence reaches to almost every corner of India—and beyond. The center has no massive clinic, no large and impressive buildings. But it is here that people come for counseling, for seminars, and for training in people-helping skills. It is here that creative approaches are being developed for reaching the poor, meeting the psychological and spiritual needs of lepers, teaching government social workers how to counsel, and giving guidance and training to church leaders. Staff members counsel every day with the patients and their families who come from great distances to the nearby Christian Medical College Hospital. There are programs for teaching communication and healing broken marriages. And staff members are developing unique counseling approaches to meet the needs and expectations of people who live in a culture that is so different from ours.[1]

On the opposite side of the world, Dr. Evelyn Wiszinckas squeezes between the mail sacks and flies to visit troubled people who are scattered in isolated villages throughout Alaska. Dr. Wiszinckas is a clinical psychologist who works, not for the church, but for the state. Her counselees are American Indians—lonely, bored, confused by rapid cultural change, lacking in self-esteem or good interpersonal skills, and often too proud to admit that they are having emotional struggles. Such people would rarely go for counseling—even if they wanted it badly. Instead, they talk with the psychologist in stores, in the post office, and sometimes in their homes. Most are poor, psychologically depressed, and spiritually empty. Many are gripped by alcoholism—a condition that has reached epidemic proportions among the native peoples in the north.

Often the little plane that links these communities is "weathered out" and unable to fly because of the snow, winds, and ice. Sometimes, the good doctor is only able to visit a village three or four times a year. When she arrives, there is no paneled office, quiet background music, or high professional fee. The psychologist does whatever she can to help. She speaks at potluck suppers, has started support groups for the families of alcoholics, and consults with local politicians. Sometimes, she works with school kids, and she even has written a community newsletter.[2]

Is this any less innovative than B. J. Prashantham's work in Vellore?

The Circle Community Center, in the inner city of Chicago, exists to "honor and serve God by reflecting His love, compassion, redemption, strength and justice." The goals clearly reflect the beliefs of those who founded the center and who work to bring psychological, spiritual, medical, and legal counseling to the people who live on Chicago's west side.

> We endeavor [says the statement of purpose] to share the Gospel in such a manner as to meet the needs of the whole person, competently and compassionately; to encourage those we serve to seek closer and more personal relationships with God; to cooperate in the development and growth of local churches through common efforts and sharing resources; to participate in the development of indigenous Christian Black leadership; to demonstrate and promote lasting racial reconciliation; to promote the growth of strong, healthy Christian families; and to cooperate in the development of the local community, economically, socially, and educationally.

Recently, the dedicated people who work at the Circle Community Center purchased an old high school. It was a big building, with a gymnasium, a 1,100-seat auditorium, 30 classrooms, and numerous offices. It also had broken pipes, falling plaster, missing fixtures, smashed windows, vandalized rooms, and a generally dilapidated interior. From all over the city and surrounding areas, volunteers appeared to clean up and remodel the building. Their theme was Psalm 127:1, "Except the LORD build the house, they labour in vain that built it" (KJV). Their motto, Nehemiah 2:18, was painted in large letters on a sign that hung inside the front entrance: "Let us start rebuilding. . . . So they began to work."

As donations and offers of help came in, the building was renovated with six hundred sheets of drywall, seven hundred lengths of electrical conduit, fifteen miles of electrical wire, three hundred gallons of paint, and much more. Now there is space for the youth program, the Christian health center, the counseling offices, the legal clinic, and the task force that seeks to restore neighborhood housing.

Is this counseling? As a form of people-helping, is it any less innovative than the work in Vellore or in Alaska?

Each of these is a new and creative approach to helping others. There are literally hundreds of similar programs, developed and operated by sensitive caring people who live in all corners of the world. Some of these care-givers are poor; others are rich. Some are professionally trained counselors; most are not. Some are members of dynamic suburban churches; others attend little missions or don't go to church at all. Some care because they are motivated to serve Christ by reaching out to others; many have little religious interest, but are intrinsically dedicated to helping the needy. All are involved in innovative approaches that go beyond traditional counseling.

PEOPLE-HELPING IN THE CULTURE

Counseling does not take place in a cultural vacuum. All effective counseling is sensitive to the society in which the counselees live.

We, who are part of highly developed, time-conscious societies, often think of counseling as a formal procedure that takes place in a professional office where fees are charged and sessions typically last for fifty minutes.

But Jesus didn't counsel that way. He lived in a Middle Eastern, rural culture where the pace was slower and time restraints were less important. Religion was prominent in those biblical times. Family ties were stronger and, unlike our jet age, the society showed little evidence of change or mobility. It is inconceivable that Jesus would have opened a counseling practice in that culture. He met the people where they were—in the streets, in their homes, at their places of worship, near their bedsides, and wherever they worked. He spoke to individuals, small groups, and huge crowds. He counseled with the poor and the rich, the young and the old, those who were close friends and others who were strangers. He talked to committed believers and challenged the religious hypocrites. The Lord's people-helping fit the needs and life-styles of the people.

Throughout the history of counseling, effective helping has always adapted in similar ways. Some of these adaptations are both fascinating and relevant to those who counsel today.

The Gheel Community

Consider, for example, the town of Gheel in Belgium. Nobody knows why it became a shrine for the mentally ill. Local residents tell of an Irish princess who came to live in a nearby forest many centuries ago. The girl was dedicated to serving the poor and helping the mentally destitute. But she was murdered by her own father and, according to the myth, was reincarnated as St. Dymphna, patron saint of the mentally ill.

As early as the thirteenth century, pilgrims came to worship at Gheel and to seek cures for their mental ills. Since there were no hotels, the local residents opened their homes. For the first time, many emotionally distraught people found security and love in stable family settings. The "patients" lived with the local residents, found jobs in the community, experienced genuine acceptance, and began to improve. Some never left.

The homes at Gheel are still open. At times, there are problems with these unusual living arrangements, but even today several hundred mental patients are living with the families

19

of Gheel. Except for a requirement that they avoid use of alcohol, these people live in the community and move about with few restrictions.

Moral Therapy

When they first began to help the mentally distraught, Gheel's residents were unlike most other communities. More typical of early treatment was a London mental "asylum" established by King Henry VIII in the mid-sixteenth century. St. Mary of Bethlehem Hospital had a name that was too long and too difficult for the local residents to pronounce. So they slurred the words together and referred to the place as "bedlam." Inmates were treated with incredible cruelty. It was widely assumed that evil spirits created madness and the cruel treatment was intended to drive the spirits away. On Sunday afternoons, the more violent inhabitants were exhibited, like animals in a zoo, to any curious Londoner who was willing to pay one penny for a look.

Into these scenes came a number of reformers, some of whom were criticized severely for advocating more humane treatment for the mentally distraught. Nevertheless, the reformers gained a slow foothold in Europe and soon their ideas crossed the Atlantic to the infant New World settlements. The first hospitals in America were cheerful, homelike places where cruel punishment and "shock treatments" were forbidden. Patients were treated with kindness, patience, and respect. Following a visit to Boston State Hospital, Charles Dickens wrote of the politeness, "good-breeding," encouragement, and self-respect that he saw, even in the most unhappy people. This treatment came to be known as *moral therapy* — a compassionate approach that instilled hope and self-confidence.[3]

Sometimes this moral therapy was given by believers. In his 1842 report to the officers of the Retreat for the Insane at Hartford, the chaplain commented on his patients' religious needs. "My increasing experience among the insane, extending now to almost four years of daily intercourse," wrote the chaplain in his somewhat flowery nineteenth-century language, "brings me to the conclusion that the consoling truths of the Gospel are most beneficently adapted by their divine Author . . . to the relief of the malady under which a deranged person labors." The chaplain went on to speak about the "comforting and hope-inspiring power" of religious truths. He noted the importance of "religious exercises" and described the therapeutic effects that come when one listens daily to the "truths and precepts of the Word of God." [4]

Nobody knows why moral treatment disappeared. Some have suggested that as hospitals grew larger, compassionate care became more difficult to provide. There were limited funds and fewer staff members, so attentive concern for patients gave way to cold institutional efficiency. The young profession of psychiatry was inclined to believe that personal problems were more medical than moral. Increasing immigration brought many stresses on the new arrivals; and soon hospitals were filled with "foreign insane paupers" [5] whose cultural backgrounds and inability to speak English made them poor candidates for moral therapy. Maybe, too, caring became less popular in America as the society became more self-centered. There is truth in the idea that the way we treat each other is often reflected in the way we treat our mentally ill.[6]

Postwar Trends

It is well known that Sigmund Freud's theories dominated psychiatric treatment during the first half of this century. Psychoanalysis is a long-term, expensive treatment technique that was popular with those who had plenty of time and money. But it wasn't very useful when the Second World War put stress on whole civilian populations and led to breakdowns among military personnel. Newer, more efficient treatment approaches had to be developed and many of these persisted and were used widely after the war ended.

The early 1950s brought even more drastic changes. The development and use of new tranquilizing drugs revolutionized psychiatric hospitals and outpatient treatment. Almost overnight it became possible chemically to reduce feelings of anxiety and depression, to eliminate many bizarre behaviors, and to help numerous people cope more effectively with their stresses. At the same time, there was a movement away from the construction of large mental hospitals and a trend toward treating people in their own communities, through clinics or psychiatric wards in local hospitals.

With increasing frequency, this treatment was influenced by *milieutherapie*, an approach that came from Germany but rapidly spread to other countries. "Let us not leave treatment to periodic interviews with professionals," the new milieu therapists stated. Instead, there were efforts to involve the entire hospital community in treatment: doctors, nurses, ward aides, physical therapists, other patients, and sometimes even the janitors and secretaries. Everybody shared responsibility for helping one another, challenging unhealthy thinking, giving encouragement, and teaching people how to cope. Individual counseling sessions were not eliminated, but their importance was deemphasized. It was a movement with characteristics that fit beautifully into the culture of postwar America. Treatment was democratic, informal, open, and inspirational. There were no white coats, nurse's uniforms, fancy titles, or other symbols of professional rank.

The advocates of milieu therapy rarely mentioned the church or its potential as a therapeutic community; their approach was intended for use in psychiatric facilities. Even in mental hospitals, however, enthusiasm for the new technique soon waned. Most professional and pastoral counselors continued to do what they have always done best: one-to-one counseling with individuals or family members who come to an office looking for help.

There will always be a need for such counseling. Although its effectiveness has been criticized, the individual therapy session appears to bring help to many people. It would be foolish and irresponsible to suggest that one-to-one counseling will or should disappear.

But individual approaches cannot meet the needs of everyone who could use help. Traditional counseling is too expensive, too time consuming, too threatening, and often too limited. It rarely works in Vellore, Alaska, or inner-city Chicago, and it probably has limited usefulness in the communities where you and I live. The counseling professions have begun to realize that individual approaches must be supplemented by other types of helping that can be adapted to the needs and cultures of people who have problems. Helpers must give more consideration to what has been called outreach in counseling: moving out of our offices both physically and psychologically to find additional ways to influence the total population.[7]

Does this sound like evangelism? Should pastoral counselors be moving away from their offices, reaching out to hurting people in their communities? Was Lawrence Crabb correct when he stated that the local church "should and can assume responsibility for restoring distressed people suffering from personal ineffectiveness to full, productive, joyful lives. In order to do so, it must develop . . . unique resources for counseling"[8]? Jesus reached out to help people where they were. His followers must do the same.

PEOPLE-HELPING IN THE COMMUNITY

Swampscott, Massachusetts, doesn't sound like an ideal place to start a revolution, but it was there in 1965 that a group of psychologists met and launched a movement known as community psychology. The conference participants were concerned about the tremendous amount of money that was being spent on the treatment of emotional disorders. They were aware of research showing that traditional psychotherapy was less effective than many had been led to believe. They suspected that treatment centered too much on individuals. It appeared that counselors had forgotten families and weren't much concerned about the social conditions that cause so many personal problems. The conference pondered why many people never came for help and why treatment rarely was begun until the problems had become severe. Why did poor people and other minorities rarely get counseling? Why, the conference participants wondered, did counselors appear to be so ineffective and irrelevant in a decade when the entire world was rocked with social unrest and upheaval?

Community Counseling

Clearly there had to be some changes in traditional counseling—changes that might even be considered revolutionary.

There was talk of preventive counseling—a new approach that would help people avoid problems or keep their present struggles from getting worse. There was interest in working with community groups to eliminate some of the social conditions that create stress. Some recognized that laypeople and other nonprofessional counselors would have to be trained to offset the manpower shortages and increasing costs of psychological treatment. It became clear that the media, schools, churches, and other community agencies would be ideal channels for programs in mental health education. Most recognized that there would have to be new, cross-cultural treatment approaches that could reach racial minorities, the poor, old people, and the uneducated. Long-term treatment would have to give way to short-term approaches; prolonged office consultations might yield to active, community-based, crisis intervention.

Perhaps it is not surprising that this new emphasis was given a name: *community counseling.*[9] It is an approach that attempts to promote mental health, prevent problems, and teach coping skills. Using a variety of techniques, it seeks to help individuals, families, social institutions, and entire communities. In contrast to more traditional approaches that use one-to-one interviews, community counseling stresses prevention, environmental change, social outreach, nonprofessional involvement, and other creative approaches that reach people who normally would not or could not come for counseling. Reaching out to lepers in Vellore, flying to visit Eskimos in remote Alaskan villages, and helping the poor in Chicago are three examples of the new counseling approach in action.

Outreach in Counseling

Over the years, the field of counseling has become increasingly complicated; it is more of a specialty that takes years to master and great skill to apply effectively. Few of us want to make a complicated field even more confusing, but if we are to help people with all of our resources, we must come to see helping in a broader perspective than before. Counseling today involves more than two people sitting in a room talking over a problem.

Figure 1 gives a picture of what counseling is likely to involve in the future. It is unlikely that any one person will be able to work in all twenty-eight "boxes" of the figure, but the more areas in which we work, the more effective is likely to be our people-helping outreach. The left side of figure 1 is a column listing seven areas of concern to community counselors: the types of problems that counselees face, the "helpees" or people whom we are trying to help, the places where we do our work, the kinds of help that are provided, the

	Traditional Remedial — — — — — — — — — — — — — — — Innovative Outreach			
	Approaches			Approaches
1. Type of Problem	Acute Problem	Felt need	Growth or developmental task	Pre-awareness
2. Receiver of Help	Individual	Formal group	Informal group	Whole community
3. Place of Help	Counselor office	School church or work place	Home or other living place	Natural environment
4. Type of Help	Helping interview	Mutual aid or other group	Self-help	Environmental change
5. Giver of Help	Professional counselors	Para-professional counselors	Lay counselors	Natural helpers
6. Methods of Help	Individual help	Group help	Formal education	Informal education
7. Duration of Help	Long-term, many sessions	Short-term/ brief therapy	Informal talks	Life-span help

(Figure 1.) The Outreach Model of Counseling
(Adapted from Chris Hatcher and Bonnie S. Brooks, *Innovations in Counseling Psychology*, p.21.)

helpers who give the help, the methods that are used, and the duration of the help-giving activities.

The boxes in the figure suggest areas where help can be given. The more traditional remedial approaches are shown in the boxes on the left of the diagram; the more innovative outreach approaches are at the right.[10]

Types of problem. Traditionally, counseling has waited until a problem is acute and the counselee is in a crisis or otherwise greatly in need of help. More innovative approaches help people when they feel a need and sense that a problem might be developing, when they want help with a growth or developmental issue (such as coping with middle age or facing retirement), or even before they are aware of a problem. Premarital counseling, for example, sometimes alerts a young couple to potential problem issues that they may never have considered.

Receivers of help. Who are we trying to help? Usually, we think of counseling as help given to individuals, but counseling can also be given in formal groups where people come specifically for help. Group therapy and divorce-recovery workshops are examples. Informal groups might include Bible study groups, family gatherings, or college classrooms where people have not come for counseling but where they get help with problems nevertheless. Sometimes, the help is given to whole communities and other large groups including church congregations, service club audiences, or television viewers.

Places of help. Traditional counseling takes place in a counselor's office, but more innovative approaches may give help in schools, churches, work settings, homes, and even "natural settings" like restaurants, beaches, and beauty shops.

Types of help. The helping interview is still an important part of counseling. As we will see in a later chapter, however, there has been an explosion of interest in mutual-aid groups such as Alcoholics Anonymous, widows support groups, or weight-reduction organizations. In addition, self-help that comes through books, articles, seminars, or personal reflection is important to many people. Help also comes when whole environments can be changed to reduce stress and improve local conditions. It is known, for example, that noise can be stress inducing. For this reason, some psychologists have joined with community groups to get changes in flight patterns near residential communities surrounding airports.

Givers of help. No longer is the psychiatrist or the licensed psychologist the only one who is competent to counsel. People in other professions—nursing, teaching, law, the ministry— do a lot of counseling, and so do trained lay counselors. Even without training, friends continue to help friends in what might be called naturalistic helping.

Methods of help. Training programs for professionals often focus on the learning of counseling skills. These training programs undoubtedly make counselors more sensitive and effective in their work. Even professionals are recognizing, however, that some people do not need intensive counseling. Many can profit from group counseling (including family counseling), formal educational programs (such as courses on mental health), and informal helping that may be given by a seminar, a sermon, a television program, or an audiocassette.

Duration of help. Some people will continue to need long-term counseling given by a trained professional. But there are others who can profit from brief therapy or from short informal discussions that may pass between friends. It could be argued that this more casual consideration of problems and challenges could continue throughout the whole span of life.

This new outreach model suggests that we are moving toward a dramatically different kind of counseling. Without abandoning traditional approaches, the new counselor will constantly be reaching out to help others with creative, innovative, community-changing approaches.[11]

The Healing Community

It is difficult to define a community. Most often, the word refers to a group of people who live in the same locality, are subject to the same laws, or have common ties, interests, values, and/or problems. A community may be like the suburban neighborhood where people rarely see or talk to each other except for an occasional wave from a distance. In contrast, a community can be a closely knit group where there is frequent contact, lively "community spirit," and a willingness to serve one another. The origins of the word reflect that spirit. The Latin *communis* consists of *com,* which means "together," and *munis,* meaning "ready to be of service." The real community is "ready to be of service together." [12]

Even as they developed individual approaches to therapy, the helping professions have recognized the healing effects of communities. Some family and community influences are so destructive that they undermine what happens in individual counseling. But we have also seen how supportive friends, relatives, and neighbors can have a tremendous therapeutic influence in the lives of those who are facing crises or going through deep distress.

Communities that bring such healing may be informal groups, such as families, or more formally organized "collectivities" who have intense commitment to the group and a common desire to find healing for psychological, behavioral, or spiritual hurts. [13] Defined in this more formal way, *the healing community is a group of people who are committed to helping one another.* Some members may have greater needs than others. Some may give more than they get. But all are committed to "being of service together."

According to psychiatrist Richard Almond, healing communities consist of fellow sufferers who value their involvement in the group and who are convinced that there is healing power within the community. [14] The group members feel accepted, encouraged, and valued even as they admit their failures, share their hurts, or are challenged because of their weaknesses. In America, we value individuality and tend to avoid intimate involvement with others. But few experiences are more therapeutic than close contact with people who care for us and who value our care in return.

PEOPLE-HELPING IN THE CHURCH

Dr. O. Hobart Mowrer was a controversial psychologist, whose brilliant research led to his election as president of the American Psychological Association, but whose unorthodox views of psychotherapy led to conflicts with his colleagues.

In an oft-quoted remark, Mowrer stated that evangelical religion had "sold its birthright for a mess of psychological pottage." [15] Although he never claimed to be a believer, Mowrer was convinced that sin was the root cause of mental illness. His lifelong struggles with severe depression had convinced him that it was the church, and not psychology, that could best lead people to forgiveness and healing. But the church, in his opinion, had been distracted from this mission by its fascination with psychology and its enthusiasm about following the teachings of Freud, "the Pied Piper who beguiled us into serious misconceptions and practices." [16]

As a psychologist, I am distressed by well-meaning but ill-informed Christians who dismiss psychology as being of no use to the church. Such attitudes rarely come from those who have studied psychology carefully and seen its potential as a people-helping tool. Equally disturbing, however, is the view that the church is little more than a therapeutic community that dispenses psychological advice and pastoral therapy. Mowrer was perceptive in his view that at least some churches have replaced their theological uniqueness with "a mess of psychological pottage."

The church was created by Christ as a dynamic witness, empowered by the Holy Spirit. Its task was—and is—to make disciples of all nations, teaching ourselves and others to obey everything that Christ commanded the disciples (Matt. 28:19, 20).

The disciples had lived with Jesus throughout his years of ministry. They had watched his lifestyle, asked questions, and heard him preach. When they were sent out on a training mission, they were given power and authority from the Lord and commanded to "preach the kingdom of God and to heal the sick" (Luke 9:2, NKJV).

Surely there can be no solid case made for the view that Jesus stressed preaching but deemphasized healing. He did both and commanded his followers to do the same. By the spoken Word and by compassionate actions, he brought people to himself and "made disciples." To be true to Scripture, the church today must have a deep commitment to preaching *and* to healing. One without the other is a distortion of the divine commission.

The church is an evangelizing, preaching, teaching, discipling, sending community. It also must be a therapeutic community where people find love, acceptance, forgiveness, support, hope, encouragement, burden-bearing, caring, meaning, opportunities for service, challenge, and help in times of need. Within the church community, people can find others who share "like precious faith" and who value the spiritual issues that secular therapists so often overlook. Few churches meet these ideals and some fail miserably.[17]

The Church and Community Counseling

In reaching their goals, could churches make use of community counseling with an outreach emphasis? Seminaries, pastors, and church members have long recognized the importance of pastoral counseling. This has traditionally been a one-to-one type of relationship, however, and only a few voices have suggested that the church should also be involved in community mental health.[18] The remainder of this book will consider practical ways by which the findings of community psychology can be adapted for use in the local church.

We will see, too, that the church can contribute much to the emerging field of community psychology. The Swampscott Conference was held only a few years ago. In contrast, the church's response to the Great Commission has led Christians to be involved with practical people-helping for centuries. Christians have been actively involved in prison reform, the abolition of slavery and prejudice, the relief of suffering, and the fight against poverty. Committed believers have built hundreds of hospitals, orphanages, relief centers, schools, and rescue missions. Dedicated Christian people-helpers have traveled literally to all parts of the world and given huge sums of money, often at considerable sacrifice and frequently with no visible rewards for their efforts. Mother Teresa is not a community psychologist, but surely community psychology could learn much from this famous Nobel Prize winner, and others, whose compassionate helping work is motivated by a desire to obey Christ and follow in his footsteps.

Psychological Megatrends

On the day when you read these words, it is estimated that approximately one thousand books are in the process of being published throughout the world. Most of these appear following long hours of lonely, painstaking work by authors who sense real satisfaction when they look for the first time at their books in print. Many hope that their books will influence thousands, but, within a year, most of these volumes will be unnoticed, unread, and collecting dust in libraries, warehouses, and discount bookstores.

Occasionally, a book will rise to the top of this pile, make a special impact, and sell millions of copies. Such was *Megatrends,* John Naisbitt's thoughtful analysis of the trends facing his country and the world in the coming years.[19] The book shows that our society is in a period of great change and outlines trends that will influence us all in the future. We can resist these changes and try holding on to the past, or we can observe what is happening and adapt our businesses, ministries, and lifestyles to meet the challenges of the evolving future.

Community counseling is one of the megatrends within the helping professions, but there are others. Already we see how increasing media influence can both create stress and help people cope. There is a new interest in counseling programs for the aged and physically ill.[20] Some specialists are adapting counseling to the work place and military environments.[21] Others are refining school and educational psychology. A few are looking for ways to meet the needs of those who have interest in the occult, mysticism, and the psychology of religion.

With increasing frequency, computers are being used as aids to counseling. They give, score, and interpret tests. Sometimes, they also counsel people who use self-help computer programs, much to the chagrin and concern of many traditional counselors. Nevertheless, some of these same counselors, now find themselves using videocassettes, booklets, creative homework assignments, and other nontraditional approaches to helping. Dr. Freud would have been shocked.

Long before the age of Freud, and centuries before the invention of computers, the apostle Paul wrote a letter about the church as a caring community. Believers must be humble, gentle, and patient, he wrote (Eph. 4:2). They must bear with one another in a spirit of love and remember that individuals have different gifts and capabilities. Within the church, God's people must be given preparation for practical service. They must be guided toward the full maturity that comes ultimately to the faithful who strive for unity and grow to maturity because of their knowledge of Jesus Christ (Eph. 4:2, 3, 12, 13).

When they want to be used by God to help others, men and women of faith are not overwhelmed by current megatrends. Throughout the centuries, and under a variety of circumstances, believers have reached out to help others, often in creative ways. It is to some of these old and new approaches that we turn our attention in the following pages.

CHAPTER TWO

PUBLIC COUNSELING

DURING THE COURSE of their convention, several years ago, members of the American Psychological Association gathered to hear the annual presidential address. The president that year, Dr. George Miller, had previously announced his topic, but probably few in the audience expected to hear much that was new or different. Convention speeches do tend to be boring!

But Dr. Miller surprised his audience by proposing that they should be giving psychology away, making it understandable, practical, relevant, and meaningful to nonprofessionals. Psychologists should stop hoarding their insights, the speaker maintained. They should translate psychological terms into popular language and find practical ways to help others use the conclusions of psychological research.

The speech ignited an explosion of controversy. Some argued that psychologists didn't have enough knowledge to "give away." Others felt that nonpsychologists surely would misunderstand or misuse the information that might be disclosed as part of the new movement.

Like most controversies, this one soon faded and died; but a premise of Dr. Miller's remained: people can, should, and do get help apart from the offices of professional counselors.

When you have a problem or face a difficult decision, where do you go for help? If you are like me, you pray about the issue and probably think of ways to help yourself. You might talk it over with your spouse, another family member, or a close friend. Perhaps you would be motivated enough to read a self-help book, listen to a cassette tape, attend a seminar, or talk things over with a pastoral counselor. If you needed professional counseling, this would probably come only after other sources of help had been tried.

A national survey, completed in the 1970s, found that more people turned to pastors for help than to any other group of counselors.[1] Many also talked with their doctors, fellow workers, family members, or personal friends.

No one knows how many people seek guidance in magazine articles or from self-help books. Talk shows, PTA meetings, banquet speeches, and sharing groups (including Bible study groups) provide other opportunities for people to get help with their problems or stresses.

Then, there is the help that comes from sermons.

It has been estimated that two hundred thousand sermons are preached every Sunday. Often, the same people return week after week to hear messages that have the potential to provide lasting help and encouragement. Preachers are usually trusted, and their sermons can have far-reaching influence. "Preach to the suffering," Joseph Parker advised in his famous statement of a century ago. "There's a broken heart in every pew." Harry Emerson Fosdick might have agreed. He saw preaching as "personal counseling on a group scale."[2]

In one of his books on counseling, Howard Clinebell suggested that

> the sermon offers a minister one of his most valuable opportunities to enhance the mental and spiritual health of his people. . . . Effective preaching offers an efficient means of helping a number of individuals simultaneously. From a mental health viewpoint, the sermon has both preventive and therapeutic potentialities. For relatively healthy persons it can stimulate personality growth and raise the general level of their creativity. It can release strength within those who are struggling with a personal crisis. It can support those whose personality foundations are weak, and motivate some who are burdened to seek professional help.[3]

Most important, it can point people to Jesus Christ, the Prince of Peace and Wonderful Counselor, who came to bring eternal life in the future and abundant life while we are here on earth.

Several years ago, I led a graduate-level seminar on the subject of how people are helped through the media and from the public platform. We studied biblical communicators and analyzed the works of more contemporary speakers and writers who appear to be effective in helping people through public ministries. Then we considered the following questions that must concern anyone who attempts to help others through speaking or writing.

WHY SHOULD WE TRY TO HELP PEOPLE PUBLICLY?

The example of Jesus gives us our most basic reason for public people-helping. He never hesitated to counsel with individuals on a one-to-one basis, but these personal conversations were set within the context of a public-speaking ministry that clearly met the needs of both small groups and large crowds of listeners.

Even in our psychologically sophisticated society, it takes courage for individuals to admit to themselves and to others that they need counseling. Probably, most people try first to solve their problems alone or with the help of a friend. Some will never be willing to seek out a counselor, but when these people attend church, they can find encouragement and guidance in the pastor's messages. There is no need for these listeners to admit to others that "the speaker is talking about my problem." The worshiper is helped without having to confess that a problem exists. For such people, public help is the only counseling they may ever get. For many, public help is all they need.

It could be argued, of course, that such secrecy is not always healthy. Isn't it better to face a problem honestly and to discuss it openly?

Before they are willing to do that, some people prefer to get to know the prospective counselor from a safe distance. These are the people who watch their pastors from week to week, building the courage to ask for face-to-face help from the one whose compassion and sensitivity have been demonstrated in the pulpit.

Even when they are willing to seek counseling, many simply cannot afford a professional therapist's fees. Government money that once supported public counseling centers is drying up and, for many, the only help available is that which comes from television screens, self-help books, magazines, and pastoral messages. Very often, local pastors are far more effective people-helpers than the advice givers who appear in the media or on speaker's platforms at weekend seminars.

How Do We Help People Publicly?

Recently, I had lunch with a Christian leader who shared his lack of respect for preachers whose lives do not reflect their messages. "When a preacher talks about ministering to the poor but lives an affluent lifestyle, there is something wrong," my friend suggested. "When a pastor preaches about evangelism but never presents the gospel to a nonbeliever, this is hypocrisy."

Most of us know of psychologists (and preachers) who conduct marriage enrichment workshops while their own marriages are falling apart. Some speakers dare to hold seminars on money management while their own finances are in chaos. It is easy, I have discovered, to be so busy writing books about caring that there is no time to care. If we hope to have an impact on lives, those of us who seek to help people publicly must consistently strive to practice what we preach.

It is not difficult to convince seminary students that preaching to human needs is important. Too often, however, these students dream of preparing their sermons from the uninterrupted quiet of a book-lined study. Encouraged by professors who model scholarship and academic excellence, and impressed by well-known public communicators, many seminarians long to become "pastor-teachers" who can prepare messages while they leave the hard realities of counseling to somebody else.

Such goals may seem attractive, but good preachers soon learn that one cannot be an effective communicator in the pulpit if one is out of contact with people. John R. W. Stott writes that biblical and theological studies are indispensable for good preaching, but they must be supplemented by a knowledge of contemporary issues.[4] That knowledge comes from newspapers, television, secular book reviews, films, plays, and anything else that mirrors the current issues in society. Even more important is personal interaction with people. By listening to their concerns and struggles, we are better able to speak and write about their needs. Preachers who know people intimately and who take counseling seriously find that this deepens their preaching.[5]

A preacher, psychologist, teacher, writer, or other communicator is unlikely to be effective in helping people publicly if he or she is interpersonally inept, insensitive to individual needs, or inclined to avoid individuals who are hurting. If you are not sensitive to people, you are not likely to be a good communicator. Of course, the Word of God is incisive and the Holy Spirit does use imperfect servants to accomplish divine purposes. The great biblical preachers were intimately acquainted with their Lord and they preached the Word of God; but these same men and women were deeply aware of human need and their messages always reflected that essential sensitivity.[6]

Characteristics of Good Public Communication

Helpful public messages, both spoken and written, should reflect the basics of good communication.[7] These basics, which include the following, are well known but often forgotten.

Correct grammar. The pulpit or other public platform is no place to display sloppy English and incomplete sentences.

Clearly understood terms. As much as possible, avoid technical words and other jargon that could be misunderstood. Even words like *self-esteem, maturity,* or *depression* may be confusing to some people.

Simplicity. Ideas should be presented in well-organized, easy-to-follow, clear ways. Complicated theories and technical words may be of interest to academicians or their students, but none of this is likely to help needy people in a congregation or an audience.

I know a man who is a marvelous orator. He speaks with a big booming voice. Lengthy, exotic, embellished words roll from his tongue, accompanied by flamboyant, ostentatious gestures. Everybody is impressed with his awesome and amazing elocution. And nobody knows what he's talking about!

Far more effective is the person who communicates with simple words and ideas. Such simplicity is not easy; it only comes with hard work and careful thinking. It is easier to use flowery language. But that confuses people and indicates that the speaker has not organized his or her thoughts clearly.

To be simple is not the same as being simplistic. The simplistic solution to a problem is unrealistic, difficult to apply, and not really practical. When we tell people to "stop worrying," for example, when we say "don't be depressed," or when we proclaim that "all problems will disappear if you just give them to the Lord," we are dispensing solutions that are both too vague to follow and too simplistic to be helpful. The helper must strive to give guidance that is clearly stated, accurate, and practical.

Relevance. We cannot expect to give help from the public platform when we are unaware of people's needs. It is pointless to answer questions that are not being asked or to give solutions to problems that nobody is facing.

There will be times, however, when the speaker must alert an audience to existing problems that are not recognized. In writing to the Corinthians, for example, Paul identified some dangers that were facing the church and pointed out that the believers were spiritual babies who needed to grow into maturity. After the problems were identified, the believers were more ready to hear the apostle's solutions.

Interest. In a recent interview, one of Hollywood's best producers mentioned that he tries to make the kind of movies that he would like to see himself. Our motives for preaching and public people-helping differ from the moviemaker's motives, but I wonder how many of us would be interested in hearing our own messages? If you sat in the pews every week, would you be bored with your sermons? Listening to tapes of your messages might help to answer that question.

Dialogue. In his book on preaching, Stott has argued that effective sermons should not be monologues.[8] Instead, the speaker should be involved in a silent dialogue with the listeners. What is said should provoke questions which the speaker then seeks to answer. Stott writes that one of the greatest gifts a preacher needs is "such a sensitive understanding of people and their problems that he can anticipate their reactions to each part of his sermon and respond to them. Preaching is rather like playing chess, in that the expert chess player keeps several moves ahead of his opponent, and is always ready to respond, whatever piece he decides to move next." [9]

Sincerity and conviction. Imagine the futility of trying to convince others of a message that you don't believe yourself. Phoniness, hypocrisy, indifference, laziness, and lack of conviction in the speaker can all lead to boredom in the audience. The best communicators are those who believe their message and are honestly and courageously committed to sharing their convictions. Such sincerity undergirds and reinforces what is said verbally.

WHAT ARE THE PROBLEMS IN HELPING PEOPLE PUBLICLY?

People who are effective in their work often discover that success stimulates opposition. When a politician, teacher, businessman, parent, or pastor is competent, it seems that criticism and misunderstanding are almost certain to arise. You can expect this to be true if you are a success in helping people from the pulpit or other public platform. The problems are likely to come from one or more of three sources: your audience, your colleagues, or yourself.

Problems from Your Audience

All speakers work on the assumption that listeners will be able to evaluate what is said and apply it to their lives. The preacher, in addition, assumes that the Holy Spirit is able to illumine the minds of those who listen and to guide them as they make changes in their thinking and behavior.

These assumptions, while valid, must be combined with the recognition that some listeners do not want to change. Their resistance, which may not even be conscious, insures that they often are untouched by a message.

Other listeners have unrealistic expectations and assume that a speaker will be able to offer almost magical solutions to problems that could have been developing for years. It may help if you state clearly what you hope to accomplish in a message or sermon series. Emphasize that some problems can't be resolved without more personal help. Even with these statements, however, some listeners won't hear your goals or your warnings. They continue to believe that your talks will sweep away their problems; and they will be disappointed and critical when their expectations are not met.

Almost as difficult is the overly enthusiastic "follower" who accepts everything you say without question. Even the apostle Paul was evaluated by the noble Bereans who listened to his message and then searched the Scriptures to see if he was correct. Surely both Paul and the Bereans were better Christians as a result of that experience.

Such careful evaluation seems to be rare today. The public communicator, therefore, must be careful to present facts accurately and to state conclusions carefully.

Even then, you may encounter another audience problem—the misinterpretation of your message. It is common for people to pull ideas out of context or to reach conclusions that were not intended by the speaker. Each listener filters a sermon through his or her grid of experience and sees the message from a personal perspective. This may explain why students in a classroom can all take notes on the same lecture, but when the notes are compared, there often is great diversity in what has been written. Opportunities for distortion are even greater when the listener is under distress and desperately searching for help.

Within every congregation there probably will be some people who are too distraught to listen carefully or to apply what has been said. In a widely publicized case, a lady was arrested several years ago and charged with child abuse after she heard a sermon on discipline and concluded that it was her duty to beat her son with a rod until he submitted to the mother's authority. It is well known that our society currently has a fascination with law suits. Might it be only a matter of time before some distraught parishioner or family member tries to bring legal action against a preacher, speaker, or writer whose advice was unclear or whose message was misinterpreted? Keeping a file of tape-recorded sermons may be wise insurance.

In this context, the parable of the sower takes on special relevance:

> Listen then to what the parable of the sower means: When anyone hears the message about the kingdom and does not understand it, the evil one comes and snatches away what was sown in his heart. This is the seed sown along the path. The one who received the seed that fell on rocky places is the man who hears the word and at once receives it with joy. But since he has no root, he lasts only a short time. When trouble or persecution comes because of the word, he quickly falls away. The one who received the seed that fell among the thorns is the man who hears the word, but the worries of this life and the deceitfulness of wealth choke it, making it unfruitful (Matt. 13:18–22).

But all is not hopeless. When we preach the Word of God, there also are those who do hear, who do understand clearly, and who do experience abundant changes and fruitfulness in their lives as a result of the message. In spite of the potential for misinterpretation, many people are regularly helped by people-helping presentations.

Problems from Your Colleagues

I am hesitant to raise this and even more reluctant to believe that the effectiveness of one speaker or writer leads others to be envious.

If you really are able to help people from the pulpit, this fact gets to be known and often (but not always) the size of the congregation begins to swell. Sometimes two or three identical worship services are necessary. This can be encouraging for you but threatening to pastors in other churches, especially if you live in a community where large congregations and multiple services have become status symbols and not-too-subtle indicators of ecclesiastical success. If your sermons are broadcast on radio, televised, or published in a book, there is even more potential for criticism.

The place to start dealing with this is on your knees before the Lord. It is difficult to keep things in perspective when, at the same time, we are criticized for our effectiveness and acclaimed for being successful. How easy it is to forget that it is God who "brings one down, he exalts another" (Ps. 75:7). It is he who gives us the voice to speak, the brains to express ideas clearly, and the opportunities to minister. Each of us is one heartbeat away from silence.

Every Christian—those who preach and those who do not, those who publish their writings and those who cannot, those with large congregations and those who minister to smaller groups in remote places—each of us must remember the penetrating words of Jeremiah:

Let not the wise man boast of his wisdom
or the strong man boast of his strength
or the rich man boast of his riches,
but let him who boasts boast about this:
that he understands and knows me,
that I am the LORD, who exercises kindness,

justice and righteousness on earth,
for in these I delight (Jer. 9:23–24).

True humility is an attitude that neither gloats over one's successes nor denies one's effectiveness. The humble person rejoices when others are effective and weeps with sincerity when others hurt. The humble communicator is able to pray sincerely for his or her colleagues, to accept and encourage them, and to ask the Lord to change all of our attitudes so we will not be proud, envious, hypercritical, or destructively competitive.

We must also recognize that critics often raise genuine questions about our messages. Such criticisms may come not from hearts of envy but from the reflections of sincere fellow believers who genuinely are concerned, lest we slip into popular advice-giving from the pulpit and move away from the clear proclamation of God's Word.

D. A. Carson has expressed this concern concisely: "There is far too little stress on God's character and the requirements of the kingdom, and far too much stress on our needs. Worse, our needs are cast in preeminently psychological categories, not moral ones." We preach about alienation and loneliness, Carson writes, but we say little about bitterness, self-seeking, or hatred. Our sermons discuss frustration and fear, but are less inclined to mention prayerlessness or unbelief. We promise joy, peace, and abundance, but we cast these in psychological terms and fail to mention that these goals ultimately come from the Lord.[10]

It is difficult to know which is worse: a psychological homily that has no biblical content or a dull theological discourse that lacks practical relevance and application. Each of these is unbalanced and likely to bring justified criticism from your colleagues.

Problems from Yourself

A famous actress was recently interviewed about her long and successful career. "I never gave a performance that satisfied me completely," she told the interviewer. "I always want to try one more time to get it right."

Is this dedication to excellence at the basis of most successful careers? Should we who serve Christ have a similar commitment to high quality in our ministries?

There is value in examining our work frequently and looking for ways to improve. I have noticed, however, that it is easy to get overly critical of my own work, to assume that I am saying nothing new, to fear that my speaking or writing is merely stating the obvious, or to be afraid that I am repeating myself and restating old illustrations. While thoughts like these stimulate me to evaluate my work and strive for improvement, they also can hinder my effectiveness. I suspect that others share similar self-evaluations.

To keep quality in our work, without undermining ourselves, each of us needs constant exposure to the probing light of God's Word and frequent discussions with an honest loving friend or two who can give more objective perspectives on our work. Try to find someone who will be honest, not someone who will like or hate whatever you do regardless of its quality.

At professional conventions, psychologists may continue to debate whether and how to offer public help to those in need; but for preachers, such debate is less necessary. Christians are called to minister to one another and this must include helping people from the pulpit. The question we face is how we can minister most effectively.

Spirit-guided, relevant, clear, Bible-based preaching that speaks to human needs has no equal as a means of helping people publicly. The availability of television and radio permits the preacher to reach a larger audience, and, for some, there is the influence that will come from writing.

No one person can communicate effectively using all of the channels that are currently available. It is helpful nevertheless to consider some of the alternative ways in which people can be helped publicly.

WHAT ARE OTHER APPROACHES TO PUBLIC PEOPLE-HELPING?

Malcolm Muggeridge is a British commentator, well known in England because of his humorous, insightful writings and radio programs. Never afraid to say what he thinks, Muggeridge has both delighted and infuriated all kinds of people, including, apparently, the queen herself.[11]

It is unlikely that the television industry was happy with his comments on the media after Muggeridge became a Christian. "The Media have provided the Devil with perhaps the greatest opportunity accorded him since Adam and Eve were turned out of the Garden of Eden," Muggeridge wrote.[12] The media in general and television in particular have exploited "the weaknesses and wretchedness of men," stimulating human carnality, greed, arrogance, power, narcissism, and debauchery "on a scale that the Prince of Darkness himself must envy."

Even with "all their power of persuasion and corruption," however, Muggeridge argues that the media "can no more keep Christ out than the Emperor Nero could keep the words of the Apostle Paul from spreading themselves throughout an already ramshackle Roman Empire." [13] Who among us has not heard of lives that were changed and people who were helped because some committed believers have creatively used the media to spread the gospel and offer spiritual healing? Despite all the criticism of television evangelists and electronic churches, it is true that there are strongly resistant and desperately hurting people who are reached only in the privacy of their own living rooms.

Electronic People-Helping

Most of us have seen the power of Pat Robertson's Christian Broadcasting Network, Billy Graham's televised crusades, Robert Schuller's "Hour of Power," or James Dobson's "Focus on the Family" films and radio programs. These are well known and highly influential, but who could estimate how many other religious programs and secular self-help broadcasts are going over the airwaves even as you read these words?

Probably many of us cringe at some of the sloppy production, poor articulation, egotistical speakers, blatant commercialism, and factual inaccuracies that characterize many Christian films, radio broadcasts, and television programs.[14] Nevertheless, electronic media present us with incredible opportunities to evangelize, inform, and educate people about mental health, and teach viewers or listeners how to cope with stress and prevent psychological disturbance.

Good media productions require careful planning, hard work, dedicated commitment, and a willingness to get guidance from competent people who are trained in making high-quality productions. The public people-helper has the challenge of stimulating interest, peaking curiosity, using everyday language, and finding ways to teach and entertain at the same time. Often, complicated ideas must be presented concisely and briefly. Great care must be taken to avoid factual errors or statements that could be misinterpreted by those who listen. Perhaps it is not surprising that professional psychologists have recently shown concern about the ethics of "media psychology" and the potential for harm.[15] There are warnings about sensationalism in the media's treatment of human problems and concern that some viewers are turning solely to television for help in grappling with their problems.[16]

Can the church be any less concerned? Helping people through the electronic media is a powerful and sobering responsibility that has potential for both harm and good. It should not be taken lightly.

In pondering this responsibility, remember that the production of major and expensive programs is not the only way to help people electronically. The recording of messages on audiocassette tapes and making these available locally is both an inexpensive and sometimes overlooked way to help others. Churches that use a "dial a prayer" or other carefully planned telephone minimessages also reach out inexpensively— twenty-four hours a day.[17]

Then there is the talk show. It is estimated that more than four thousand interview programs are broadcast daily throughout the United States and Canada. These include news features, public service programs, interviews, and talk shows, all of which need guests. It isn't easy to get on the big network talk shows, but local producers are often looking for bright, articulate people who can speak clearly and intelligently. Watch your local media and then let the stations know of your availability if you see this as one way to help.[18] Such appearances can give useful help and indirectly stimulate interest in the speaker's church and counseling ministry. In this way, people are contacted who might never be reached in any other way.

Seminar People-Helping

Several years ago, the evangelical and secular worlds were both amazed by the success of a quiet midwestern bachelor named Bill Gothard whose one-man monologue seminars filled huge auditoriums, even with no advertising. Critics found fault, but the Gothard phenomenon rolled on. Followers continued to attend the seminars, sometimes repeatedly, even after the speaker began to appear on videotape rather than in person.

Bill Gothard was sincere, creative, and practical. He put demands on his listeners, expected them to attend seminars for six evenings and all day Saturday, and challenged them to change their behavior, Christian commitment, and lifestyles. Is it surprising that a flood of Christian seminars followed in the wake of the Gothard successes?

Seminars, of course, are not new, and neither are they uniquely Christian. Business and professional seminars have long been popular, and a host of speakers regularly crisscross the continent delivering talks on a variety of subjects. As the seminar phenomenon has become more common (and more expensive), it appears that participants have become less satisfied with poor content, less inclined to settle for speaker monologues, and more demanding of dynamic entertaining presentations, preferrably accompanied by bright visual aids and high-quality "handouts."

There are two obvious ways in which you can help people through public seminars. You can conduct seminars yourself, or you can invite someone else to present a seminar in your community.

Before launching a seminar program, give careful, prayerful thought to the subject matter of your presentations and to the "market" where you plan to speak. People get tired of seminars after a while, and they may be less interested in attending your seminar than you are in giving it. Recognize that there are "fad" topics—like parenting or time management—and popular national speakers that capture public attention for a while and, to some extent, determine how people in a given community will respond to a new seminar announcement.

If you decide to go ahead with your planning, prepare your subject matter carefully and accurately. Give attention and funding to quality visual materials, and try out your ideas in front of live audiences before you "go on the road." Get feedback and ask yourself the potentially threatening question: "Would I devote a Saturday listening to a speaker like me?" Get answers from people who may be more objective and honest than your spouse or your mother.

As every public speaker knows, seminars involve a lot more than standing in front of an audience and speaking. First, you have to get the audience there. That involves advertising, working with local arrangements people, finding an auditorium, planning travel, determining costs, and making decisions about book tables, audio-visual aids, taping, and coffee breaks. Often the results are worth all of this effort, but seminars tend to be harder to plan than we first realize. And how will you feel if you work for months on the planning and discover that only twelve people show up? Small crowds aren't always bad, but they can be disappointing.

Perhaps you will find it easier to bring in an outside speaker who can lead a seminar in your church or community. Once again, you must ask whether local people will attend the seminar when it is arranged. Is the seminar speaker and the topic likely to be of interest? Can it be publicized effectively? Are people too busy to attend? Will some be unwilling to attend if you select a topic that is too threatening? Some people, for example, will stay away from a "marriage clinic" or "How to Handle Stress" seminar because they don't want others to think they have sick marriages or uncontrollable stress.

National speakers often have carefully planned seminar arrangements policies that give clear directions to the local seminar sponsor. They can tell you, for example, how much the speaker expects to be paid, whether or not hotel accommodations are desired, whether taping is permitted, what kind of audience is expected, and who absorbs the advertising and other costs if the meeting is poorly attended.

None of this is meant to discourage you from planning seminars. Often these provide great practical help for all who attend, bring nonbelievers to Christ, and strengthen the local church. When considering seminars, church leaders must honestly consider why the seminar should be held, and whether there are other, more effective ways of giving help.

Written People-Helping

One other source of help is that which comes through print. The Bible, of course, is the written Word of God and the only authoritative book for giving divine help. In this information age, however, there are literally thousands of other useful books and articles that deal with personal problems. Perhaps most counselors recommend books or articles periodically, and counselees frequently are helped.

Should you add to these publications by writing yourself? Only you can answer that question, but several considerations might guide you in your thinking.

Let us begin with the realistic but discouraging news that it is difficult to get into print. Literally thousands of writers are actively producing articles and books, most of which will never be published.[19] Writing is hard lonely work that takes more self-discipline, persistence, digging for facts, and rewriting than most people realize. It is frustrating to spend hours on a pet writing project, only to have your work greeted with numerous impersonal rejection slips.

Even when words do get into print, they often are unnoticed, unheeded, and ignored. With the proliferation of books in this country, few people see their works on bestseller lists or get healthy royalty checks. Most books sell poorly, get little promotion from publishers, and fail to have the influence that an author might like.

It cannot be denied, however, that many people get help from books or articles. If you decide to write, in spite of the difficulties, pray constantly that you will have sensitivity, depth, clarity, and quality in your work and the discernment to know what to say and how to say it.[20]

Recognize that you are not likely to be an effective writer unless you are an avid reader. Read the Bible. Read as much as you can about your topic. Read other writers to learn how they express themselves in words. Read about people and about contemporary events so you can keep your writing relevant. Read books on how to write well and how to accomplish the difficult task of getting your book or articles published.[21]

Then practice and persist. Good writing is a skill like playing the piano or figure skating. If you don't practice, you don't perform well. If you don't persist and keep writing, even when you don't feel like it, you are unlikely to produce manuscripts that can really help people.

Whatever your approach, people-helping can be demanding work. It can also be rewarding work that need not be limited to the counseling room. In a real sense, the church was "giving psychology away" long before Dr. Miller gave his presidential address. The church's "psychology" has not been the professional information that characterizes modern science. Nevertheless, by preaching, teaching, holding conferences and seminars, broadcasting, and writing, the church leader (including the professional Christian counselor) continues to have unusual opportunities for helping people find answers to their questions. Despite its weaknesses, public helping is one of the most effective ways to help people cope with their stresses.

CHAPTER THREE

MUTUAL AID AND SELF-COUNSELING

NOBODY KNOWS how long the old guide had been taking groups of tourists down the Tigris and Euphrates river banks. He'd been hired in Baghdad and talked incessantly as he adroitly led the stately camels alongside the waters of those ancient rivers. According to a visitor from Philadelphia, who later described the experience in many public lectures, the guide felt it was his duty to entertain with "stories curious and weird, ancient and modern, strange and familiar." If the visitors got bored and stopped listening, the old Arab would lose his temper, wave his well-worn cap in the air—and tell another story.

One day he announced that the time had come to share a

tale reserved only for his "particular friends." It was about Ali Hafed, a prosperous Persian, who lived near the River Indus and owned a large farm overflowing with productive orchards, grainfields, and gardens.

One day, the farmer met an ancient Buddhist priest who told Ali Hafed about diamonds. "Own one," the priest said, "and you can buy the country. Own a mine of diamonds, and your children will be on thrones of power because of their wealth."

When Ali Hafed heard about the diamonds and how much they were worth, he went to bed a poor man. He had not lost any of his possessions, but he was poor because he was discontent. Soon he sold his farm, collected the money, left his family in charge of a neighbor, and went in search of diamonds.

He never found them.

His search took him throughout Europe, and at last he stood on the shore of the bay in Barcelona. Poor, afflicted, suffering, discouraged, and miserable, he cast himself into the waters, sank beneath the incoming surf, and was never seen again.

The old Arab guide stopped the camel, adjusted the luggage, and paused to see if the visitor from Philadelphia was still listening. Clearly, there was more to the story.

Back in Persia, the man who had purchased Ali Hafed's farm found a diamond. At first, he thought it was simply an unusual stone, but the local priest knew immediately that this was a precious gem. Together, the two men rushed to dig in the sand, and thus was discovered the mine of Golcanda, the most magnificent diamond mine in the history of mankind.

"There's a moral to this story," said the Arab, again swinging his hat in the air. "Had Ali Hafed remained at home and dug in his own cellar, or underneath his own wheat fields, or in his own garden, instead of wretchedness, starvation, and death by suicide in a strange land, he would have had 'acres of diamonds.' For every acre of that old farm, yes, every shovelful, afterward revealed gems which since have decorated the crowns of monarchs." [1]

Russell Conwell, the man from Philadelphia, retold that old guide's story hundreds of times. The application was always the same: before you run off looking for wealth, security, and help in other places, look first for the potential in your own back yard.

In searching for happiness and solutions to problems, many people run (or are referred) to expensive professionals and in-depth counselors. Often, these specialists are both necessary and helpful. But in this escape to the experts, we sometimes fail to notice that there are valuable helpers in our own neighborhoods, families, and churches. These overlooked, nonprofessional people-helpers are like precious gems. In terms of bringing help and happiness, they can be far more valuable than acres of diamonds.

PEOPLE IN SYSTEMS

It has been said often than no person is an island, completely alone in the universe. Even when there were no fellow human beings, Adam communicated with God. Even when individuals choose to become hermits, they are not able to escape completely from a world that is populated by people and polluted by their carelessness.

Human beings are all influenced by what some writers have called "social systems." Defined simply, a system is a group of people who are banded together in some way and who often hold common values or beliefs. Each of us is influenced by a variety of systems. These may be recognized or completely invisible, but they affect us nevertheless.

Consider, for example, how you spent last Sunday afternoon. It is probable that your interests, your responsibilities, and the state of your health had some bearing on what you did. But your actions may also have been influenced by your:

• family system—whether the family does things together on Sundays or whether each member is occupied with independent activities;

• local community system—whether Sundays are for group activities, for working in the yard, or for everyone going separately to the beach or to a ball game;

• geographic system—whether you are in the wintry north or the sunny south;

• economic system—whether your job demands that you

work on Sundays, or whether you are able to take the day off;

• your local marketing system—whether shopping centers are open on Sundays or whether most stores are closed;

• your religious system—whether you are Jewish, Seventh-Day Adventist, Baptist, Catholic, committed believer, minimally involved with religion, or agnostic;

• your friendship system—how many friends you have, how much they influence your behavior, and how they spend their afternoons on Sunday; and

• your value system—how you feel about shopping, working, worshiping, or playing on the Lord's Day.

No one system completely determines behavior, although for each of us, some systems are more important and influential than others. If you move to a different community, get married, change some of your values, find new friends, or are converted, it is likely that your systems (and hence your Sunday afternoon activities) will change.[2]

Figure 2 is a view of the world that most of us inhabit. At the center are the *personal systems* that include groups of fellow workers, other students (if you are in school), family members, and peers. Sometimes, one of these systems may be boring or discouraging (work, for example), but an individual can cope successfully with this if other systems are satisfying. When a man has a fulfilling marriage and feels productive in his church work, he can put up with a dull job.[3] Personal systems may also include neighborhood influences, one's Bible study group, fellow swimmers at the Y, local beauticians and merchants, or any other system that is nearby and influential.

Less intimate are *institutional systems.* Our lives are influenced daily by the government (including politicians, local authorities, and police), current economic conditions, the mass media, and social institutions such as community schools, hospitals, churches, unions, professional organizations, and clinics.

The outer circle of Figure 2 shows the *cultural systems.* These include a society's accepted beliefs, standards of right or wrong, and prevailing attitudes toward religion, education, freedom, immorality, social welfare programs, patriotism, po-

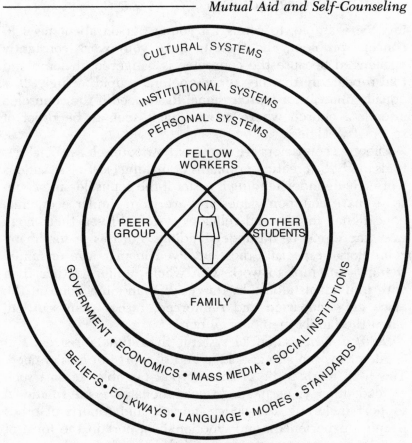

(Figure 2.) The Individual in Social Systems
(Adapted from Gerard Egan and Michael A. Cowan, *People in Systems*, p.116.)

litical activism, family stability, social class, lifestyle, credit-card buying, success, and similar issues.

Systems and Counseling

Support systems influence all of us in two ways. The systems can be harmful—creating and accentuating problems—or the systems can be helpful, powerful forces for healing and the prevention of problems.

Harmful systems. Most counselors have sometimes seen their work undermined by the influence and attitudes of a counselee's friends, family, or church members. It is frustrating, for example, to counsel a young person about his self-concept problem, and then to have your work constantly challenged because the counselee is badgered at home and told repeatedly that he is incompetent, stupid, or ugly. It is equally difficult for a professional to succeed if the counselee attends a church where counseling is seen to be proof of spiritual weakness.

Effective counselors are aware of how counselees' social systems might be creating problems or making existing situations worse. Such understanding is easier if the counselor and counselee share common values and are from similar economic, educational, family, and religious systems. Even then, however, there may be misunderstandings. For this reason, many counselors—especially those involved in marriage or family therapy—attempt to work with whole families rather than with individuals alone. In this way, counseling done in the office gets rehearsed and reinforced, rather than scuttled, when the family members go home.[4]

Helpful systems. Social systems that stimulate stress and create chaos can also give help and support in times of need. This help tends to be of three types: tangible support such as food, money, or needed accommodations; informational support including knowledge, advice, and reports of other people's experiences; and emotional support in the form of encouragement, reassurance, and the knowledge that somebody cares and is available to help.[5]

For many, there is no better support system than the family. While some families create perpetual tension, many others give encouragement, reinforce values, show love and loyalty, provide acceptance, prepare family members for future stresses, and serve as a haven and resting place away from the other pressures of life. In our mobile society, when relatives frequently are scattered geographically, distant support can come through telephone calls, and family members who live in the same house can help each other.[6]

For many, the church is also a place of support. Christians have recognized this for centuries, but professional counselors often overlook the help that comes from believers who seek to care for one another and bear each other's burdens (Gal. 6:2). By their very nature, religious institutions and people tend to stimulate support and trust among individuals, families, and neighbors. The church is "an important community resource that is underestimated and underutilized by community mental health agencies." [7] Clinebell writes that the church is a "sleeping giant, a huge potential of barely tapped resources for fostering mental health." [8]

Committed believers know this. Recently, I attended a farewell dinner for a couple who had long been active in their church and whose work was taking them to a different community. For almost an hour, members of the audience rose and gave examples of how this couple had helped in times of grief, sickness, financial struggles, loneliness, and other needs. Without this unassuming help from within the church system, many in the congregation would have had far greater difficulty in coping with their life stresses.

The church reinforces values, models desired behavior, serves as a buffer from the pressures of life, provides stability, and gives encouragement, practical help, care, love, moral standards, hope, meaning, and support, especially in times of suffering. The Scriptures repeatedly encourage believers to support the timid, help the weak, provide for the needy, and care for the distressed.

The effective counselor attempts to unite the insights that come in the counseling sessions with the support that comes from the counselee's family, church, and other supportive social systems. Together, the counselor and counselee must determine where there are useful support systems within the community, and how these can help.

In most communities, there are four sources of help within the various systems. Three of these—social networks, mutual aid groups, and self-help programs—can be like those acres of diamonds—valuable, available, and waiting in the community to give encouragement and practical help. The fourth—exotic helpers—is like fool's gold. They look attractive, capture the attention of many, and may give temporary help; but in the end, they often do more harm than good.

SOCIAL NETWORKS

Have you ever considered how many people in this country might be homeless? How many of our fellow human beings walk the streets because they have no place to go, or huddle in doorways of abandoned buildings, often clutching all of their worldly possessions in torn paper bags? These people can never take baths. Often they are hungry, cold, and lonely. A government report estimates their numbers at three hundred fifty thousand; advocates for the homeless put the number closer to three million. Perhaps half, or more, are afflicted with serious mental illness.

In urban centers, the "lucky" ones find their way into single-resident occupancy (SRO) hotels. Dilapidated and poorly maintained, these buildings often are located in rundown neighborhoods, where few local residents are left to complain about the noisy or erratic behavior of hotel tenants. Everyone is poor, there are few social activities, and many are former psychiatric patients. Nevertheless, a surprising number manage to get along from day to day without counseling or rehospitalization.

The reason, apparently, is that SRO tenants help one another. Often they cluster together in pseudo-family groups, frequently under the leadership of a dominant woman acting as a mother who nurtures, encourages, guides, and controls those in her "family." By sharing in adversity, accepting odd behavior, and making few demands on each other, these marginal people cope with life and survive.[9]

Informally, they are linked together in "social networks." A social network is a group of people who stick together often because of some common need or interest. Usually, a network forms spontaneously, serves as an enduring support system, is taken for granted, gives guidance and encouragement during times of stress, facilitates the sharing of ideas or information, and frequently has the psychological resources to help people cope successfully with the problems of living.[10]

Counselors have studied a variety of networks in addition to the SRO tenants. Prisoners, adolescents, mental patients, the terminally ill, widows, students, groups of professionals, housewives, ministers—almost all of us are involved in social networks. These networks give at least six types of help:

- material aid, such as money or other tangible assistance;
- physical help, usually in the form of "lending a hand" to accomplish tasks;
- intimate interaction, which most often involves listening while others express their feelings and personal concerns;
- guidance, including the giving of advice;
- feedback, which involves providing individuals with information about themselves; and
- social participation, such as relaxing together, having fun, and engaging in diversionary activities.[11]

From a practical point of view, there are three ways by which the counselor can make use of social networks to help counselees.

Using Existing Networks

Researchers have found that people are better able to resolve tension when they know that there are friends who care. Even if these friends are never contacted, it still is strengthening to realize that help can be available if it should be needed. When counselees know that networks exist, counseling is likely to be more successful.[12]

People who come for help often feel that they have few or no supporters. It can be beneficial, therefore, to ask counselees to name all of the people with whom they have had contact during the past year. The resulting lists often include family members, neighbors and friends, fellow employees, church members, recreational friends, teachers, doctors and dentists, barbers, waitresses, local merchants, and others. Counselees can then be asked to put a letter next to the names of those who offered advice (A), feedback (F), and support (S).

Next, you can encourage counselees to explore ways by which they could gain strength from the people whose names are on the social network list. Who could help with a job search or give information about careers? Who are the people that always stand by and make one feel happy? Who might give temporary help if necessary? With whom could the counselee spend more or less time? In what specific ways could these network people assist in meeting needs or resolving a problem? This questioning, which some have called "networking," is a means to get counselees involved with others who can help.

The church that is a caring, encouraging, loving body of believers, provides a ready-made network both for church members and for those who are outsiders. "As we have opportunity," Paul wrote to the Galatian Christians, "let us do good to all people, especially to those who belong to the family of believers" (6:10). In bringing help during times of stress, the Lord frequently works through the supportive actions of committed believers.

Stimulating Social Networks

Counselors can stimulate existing social networks to make them more caring. Hairdressers, waitresses, and bartenders, for example, listen to a lot of people's problems. These people often are trusted and, with some training, could provide even greater support for isolated, lonely people.[13] Programs already exist to train police officers in techniques of crisis intervention. Students have been found to be excellent helpers for fellow students, for hospitalized schizophrenics, for newly released patients, and for younger people who need a "big brother or sister."

Community volunteers have long provided practical help, and more recent programs to involve the elderly in helping activities have met with great success. Retired people often have the time and experience to contribute significantly to the community, sometimes as foster grandparents to retarded, physically ill, and other needy children.

The church can be involved in these and other activities. Members of congregations already help newcomers get settled in the community, provide "meals on wheels" for shut-ins, and organize blood drives. Those who live near colleges or military bases often discover that there are students or armed forces personnel who are away from their loved ones and deeply appreciate home-cooked meals and the warmth of a caring family. Such contacts provide excellent opportunities for evangelism, helping, and the compassion that Jesus both modeled and commanded. Would Christ also have reached out to those homeless people in our inner cities? None of this is traditional counseling, but it can be effective people-helping.

Creating New Networks

Overseas Christian Servicemen's Centers (OCSC) is an organization that has a concern for military personnel and their families. Scattered throughout Europe, Asia, and America, this mission (and others like it) establishes home-like centers, usually staffed by families, and most within walking distance of U.S. military bases. Service personnel are invited to drop by for meals, recreation, Bible studies, rest, informal counseling, and other nonmilitary activities. Over the years, many have found these centers to be home away from home. The center directors and their children have become substitute families for lonely service men and women and their dependents.

In visiting many of these centers, I have been impressed with the difficulties of the work and with the tremendous impact that the centers provide. Financed almost totally by donations, these centers provide a powerful supportive social network for military personnel who are away from home.[14]

Churches have limited resources and church members have limited time, but we all know of needs within our communities and around the world. When Christians are involved in outreach programs, we have unlimited opportunities for helping others, for evangelism, for discipling believers, and for preventing problems that might otherwise arise.

Ours is a changing society where people move often and where emotional closeness is frequently lacking. It has been shown scientifically that changes are handled best by people who have a variety of social networks. According to one study, "The loss of a husband or wife, the separation from one's family, the isolation from one's friends, community, or country, the frustration of apparently important desires or the failure to attain apparently important goals produced no profound or lasting reaction" in people who had solid social networks. When established relations were disrupted, these people shifted to other relationships and were able to go on.[15]

The creation and use of social networks is an important, but often neglected, aspect of pastoral people-helping.

MUTUAL-AID GROUPS

Almost everyone has heard of Alcoholics Anonymous and its thousands of chapters throughout the world. Most of us know about Weight-Watchers, Overeaters Anonymous, or Parents Without Partners. But have you heard of Candlelighters (for parents of children with cancer), Compassionate Friends (for bereaved parents), Families Anonymous (for the families of young people who have behavior problems), Gamblers Anonymous (for compulsive gamblers), Mended Hearts (for those who have had heart surgery), Recovery, Inc. (for former mental patients), Good Beginnings (for parents of premature babies), or Reach to Recovery (for women who have had mastectomies)?

These groups are all part of an explosive movement that, in the United States alone, involves an estimated fifteen million people who meet in more than five hundred thousand groups.[16] Sometimes called "self-help groups," [17] they enable members to cope with almost every conceivable human problem: widowhood, sickness, joblessness, drug abuse, life transitions, self-control, spiritual immaturity, and many more. John Naisbitt identifies this as one of the ten major movements shaping our society today,[18] and some professionals have concluded that this "nonprofessional revolution" has emerged as our primary source of mental health care.[19]

Groups like these are not new. John Wesley's fervent devotion to evangelism led to programs of social reform and the formation of Methodist Class Meetings, where people gathered in small groups for regular times of prayer, reading, and sharing. Earlier in this century, a Lutheran minister named Frank Buchman founded the Oxford Group movement. It spread rapidly, based on the conviction that all people are sinners in need of change, and that group members should meet together for mutual confession and prayer. Paul Tournier, the famous Christian counselor from Switzerland, was greatly influenced by this small group movement; [20] and O. Hobart Mowrer, the American psychologist, was so enthusiastic about groups that he enthusiastically urged "everyone . . . to be in a mutual aid or peer group (for the bearing and sharing of 'one another's burdens') not only as 'therapy' but as a way of life." [21]

Mutual-aid groups are usually small bands of people who meet voluntarily to share similar experiences and to help one another cope with common problems. The group members share common beliefs, often have been unable to get satisfactory help from professionals, and sometimes are committed to bringing social change through lobbying and other advocacy activities. There is frequently a high level of involvement by the members, an open attitude about personal pain or weaknesses, and a belief that nonprofessionals can help one another. "I've been there," many members conclude. "I know what it's like and am convinced that I can help others to cope and avoid what I went through." [22]

Mutual-Aid Groups and the Church

Church leaders are often aware of the weaknesses of mutual-aid groups. Sometimes they stimulate unrealistic hope and prevent members from getting needed medical and other professional treatment. The groups may encourage unhealthy dependence; and at times, there can be an insensitive blaming of one another when members fail to get better. There is little mention of sin in most of these groups, and so much emphasis is on self-help and mutual aid that trusting in God is deemphasized or ignored.

Nevertheless, many groups are effective and church members do find help in meetings with like-minded sufferers, regardless of theological beliefs. Parents of Murdered Children, for example, is a group that began in 1978 and now has chapters across the nation. Committed believers could well find and give solace in such a group, without compromising their Christian beliefs or withdrawing from the local church. The Christian counselor should be familiar with community mutual-aid groups and can encourage people to join, provided that the groups are not anti-Christian and assuming that they give specialized help that might not be available within the church.

Church members can also establish their own groups within the body. Bible study and sharing groups are common in churches today, and it is not unusual to find Christian versions of Alcoholics Anonymous, Parents Without Partners, or Widow-to-Widow programs.[23] As we have seen, when the church is functioning as a burden-bearing, caring community, mutual-aid groups and informal helping are likely to appear spontaneously, without waiting for the development of more formal programs.

Several years ago, a teenager in our community accidentally lost her hand in the meat grinder at a fast-food restaurant where she worked. The girl was rushed to the hospital, and members of her church immediately began their support of the family with prayer, encouragement, preparation of meals, and offers of other tangible assistance. Nothing was more helpful, however, than the appearance of a family of strangers who came to the hospital with their son. He had lost a hand several years previously, had gone through the emotional and physical readjustment along with his family, and was living a useful, productive life. The support from that visiting family was an expression of mutual aid that no counselor could hope to match.

SELF-HELP

Not long ago, I received a brochure describing a collection of self-help books and tapes that were guaranteed to change my life and bring peace of mind. There were tapes to eliminate fear and worry, build self-confidence, control stress, manage time, change personality, overcome impotence, increase personal productivity, develop assertiveness, and teach hypnosis. There were self-help aids to help people lose weight, stop smoking, overcome shyness, lower blood pressure, alleviate tension, improve vision, cope with jealousy, interpret dreams, and even "use reincarnation awareness to improve your life."

Are you skeptical about the effectiveness of these tapes?

If so, you have joined a number of professional psychologists who are uncomfortable about the claims of those who sometimes become famous and prosperous by marketing what has come to be known as "pop psychology." Father Andrew Greeley was one of the first to warn against the dangers as "wave after wave of psychological fads washed up on the shores of American culture." In their efforts to find shortcuts to peace, joy, holiness, and true happiness, many people put their faith in unproven therapeutic experiences and the pat formulas of self-help books.[24] Even church members have jumped on the bandwagon with their collections of cassette tapes and their shelves of self-help books.

As we have seen, however, tapes, books, films, and other self-help aids are not always harmful. Many people can and do get help by pondering the messages that come through the writings and recorded talks of others. At times, almost all of us benefit from the insights of those who have shared their observations and conclusions.

There can also be value in grappling with problems alone. Many people do this through journal keeping.

Some of history's greatest saints kept diaries in which they recorded daily happenings, new insights, and spiritual struggles. A journal can be a tool for self-discovery, a record of newly discovered spiritual truths, a safety valve for diffusing emotions, a place to set goals and work out plans for the future, a summary of personal reactions and observations, and a training ground for writers. Several writers have suggested that keeping a journal can be a therapeutic experience that often leads to new insights and changed behavior.[25] Although journal keeping is usually done privately, counselors sometimes suggest that counselees should talk about their journal entries in counseling sessions.

Self-Help Books

Some people would prefer to deal with their problems by seeking solutions in books. The phenomenal sales of these books suggest that many people believe the books are helpful. They certainly are cheaper than professional therapy, and often the books do give insights, practical advice, encouragement, and large doses of hope. In the opinion of psychiatrist Silvano Arieti, the best-selling books are those that promise a great deal, are easy to understand, and leave the reader feeling that the book's promises have been at least partially fulfilled.[26] The most popular self-help books appear to be written in a breezy style, filled with interesting case histories and inspiration, overflowing with how-to-do-it prescriptions, and implying that improvement will come quickly and easily. There are books that "will confirm what you wish to confirm, articulate what you want articulated and rationalize what you want rationalized, all in the name of a recognized 'authority.'"[27]

Do the books help? Professionals are not sure, especially since there rarely is research to back up the exhorbitant claims of some publishers and authors. Many books tend to encourage self-centered attitudes and create unrealistic expectations about the meaning of success or happiness. Many readers cannot or do not apply the author's principles, and sometimes there is guilt and self-condemnation because the expected changes did not occur. Other people appear to hide from their real problems by reading one optimistic self-help book after another—without making any effort to change. Then, there are those who misinterpret or misuse the author's advice, convinced nevertheless that they are applying valid psychological and/or biblical principles.

Some critics have argued that self-help books distort the public image of psychology, misuse and misinterpret Scripture, undermine American norms, and too often are designed to "make a quick buck" for authors who are "peddling snake oil remedies in books" instead of in bottles.[28] These criticisms could apply equally to many of the self-help (and overpriced) cassette tapes that some people hear in their cars and homes.

We must be careful not to throw out all self-help books and tapes because some are in error or because some users misinterpret the messages. In many respects, the Bible is a self-help book. Unlike all others, it is the Word of God, but it still is misinterpreted and misapplied, even by sincere readers.

Every counselor knows that good books and tapes can be an excellent adjunct to therapy. Almost all of us have been helped by these aids, and instead of dismissing books and tapes, it is wiser to choose and recommend them carefully. Ask yourself some basic questions.[29] Who has written the book or made the tape? What are the author's qualifications for giving advice? What can we assume about the publication, based on what we know about the publisher? What is the evidence that the material is valid and really works to bring change? Do we know that the advice is consistent with biblical teaching and psychological findings? Is it possible to put these principles to work in a practical way?

You might want to begin by asking these questions about the book that you are reading now. It might be considered a self-help book for those who want to be better counselors.

EXOTIC HELPERS

Not long ago, a large sign with a half moon was erected on the lawn of a home several blocks from where I live. The sign announced the services of a psychic healer who would give advice, read palms, and make predictions about the future.

Apparently, my neighbor is among those thousands of exotic helpers who mix superstition, religion, ritual, optimism, and sometimes occultism into a variety of healing formulas that attracts thousands. Most of these helpers charge fees for their services and are free from the cost and inconvenience of having to purchase a license to practice their arts. Professionals complain that the exotic helpers distract people from more traditional medical, psychological, and spiritual counseling. And there is evidence that some of these exotic healers are deceptive charlatans who prey on the fears, superstitions, and pocketbooks of troubled people.

In contrast, others sincerely believe that they are offering a useful service to the community. Among the poor, and some ethnic groups, exotic healers are powerful and greatly trusted. So effective is their influence that some professionals have attempted to enlist cooperation from healers whose potions and incantations are used along with established medical procedures.[30] Even when there is no collaboration with professionals, many of the exotic helpers *do* help their followers to get better.

Almost everybody has heard of the placebo effect. When people believe that a treatment will work, it often does— even when the treatment comes from a palm reader or dispenser of herbs. The exotic healers often instill hope and show the concern and caring that many hurting people are unable to find elsewhere.

Before he became a Christian, automaker John DeLorean regularly met with a "palm reader and advisor" named Sonja, who listened to his problems and constantly reassured him that all was well, even though his multimillion-dollar company was collapsing. DeLorean placed his hope and faith in Sonja who claimed to have spiritual understanding and who gave the only support and encouragement that the car manufacturer could find.[31]

Was Sonja involved in the occult? Perhaps we will never know; but Christians do not take such possibilities lightly. The Bible teaches that the world is influenced by powerful supernatural forces of evil (Eph. 6:12). The devil is a deceiver who may look attractive and helpful while he masquerades as an angel of light (2 Cor. 11:14). Undoubtedly, he traps many through the powers of exotic helpers. Sometimes these "helpers" even work with wealthy clients who live in the suburbs. Do they also trap church members who sometimes seek help from novel, professionally unqualified advice-givers who are outside the body of Christ?

Clearly, the Christian people-helper is not alone in attempting to help those in need. The counselor works within the social system of his or her community and can be aided by a variety of social networks, mutual-aid groups, and self-help techniques. These are the acres of diamonds that can assist in our counseling. To overlook their influence is to ignore a powerful healing force. To not see the harmful and deceptive forces that also inhabit the community is an equally tragic mistake.

Recently, there has been great interest in another powerful healing resource in the church and community: the effectiveness of trained lay counselors. This is the topic that we will consider in the next chapter.

CHAPTER FOUR

LAY COUNSELING

IT WAS A CREATIVE EXPERIMENT—the kind of story that newspapers love.

Two psychologists had rounded up forty male students at a well-known seminary [1] and asked them to participate in a study on careers in the church. After completing a questionnaire on religious beliefs, each student was asked to walk across campus to record a short, impromptu speech in a recording studio. Some of the students had been asked to give a speech on the Good Samaritan; others expected to talk about career concerns for ministers.

As they left for the other building, the students were given different send-offs. Some were hurried. "Oh, you're late," the researcher exclaimed. "They were expecting you a few minutes ago. We'd better get moving." Others were simply given directions to the recording room, and still others were told casually that they had lots of time and might even have to wait for a few minutes when they arrived.

As each student left the building, he came upon a "victim" coughing and slumped against the wall. As the student approached, the victim (who must have been a very good actor) closed his eyes and stopped moving.

Sixty percent of the students walked by without stopping. Of those who were in a hurry, 90 percent failed to stop. Some literally stepped over the slumped body as they hurried to give a speech about the Good Samaritan.[2]

Perpetual rushing is part of the Western way of life. Preoccupation with work and goals can easily make us insensitive to people. Even professional "Samaritans" can get so busy with counseling that we fail to notice obvious human need. We can think about theology or theories of psychology and become so absorbed with our ideas that we lose contact with individuals and their struggles.

The Bible never gives the impression that Jesus was in a hurry. Often he was pressured by people and surrounded by crowds, but he always had time to stop and help. His life and teaching emphasized face-to-face contact, and he encouraged mutual caring among his followers.

The writers of the Epistles used the words *one another* almost sixty times, usually in the form of admonitions to care, encourage, edify, teach, confront, and support. James defined *pure and undefiled religion* in terms of both holy living ("keeping oneself unstained by the world") and compassionate service, such as caring for needy widows and orphans. Throughout the Scriptures, people-helping is not proposed as an option—it is commanded as a requirement for all believers.

Over the centuries, Christians have taken this biblical mandate seriously. It is not surprising that recent secular interest in lay counseling has attracted the attention of churches. Almost everyone agrees that the needs are overwhelming and that counseling laborers are few. Professional counselors are expensive and pastoral counselors tend to be overworked. Could lay people in the church be trained more effectively to care for one another and bear one another's burdens?

Initially, this idea was shocking to many trained counselors.[3] Wouldn't well-intentioned but poorly trained lay counselors hurt more people than they would help? Wouldn't these lay helpers be offering a "watered-down" type of therapy? Was it possible that the presence of lay counselors would lure business away from professionals? And where was the evidence that minimally trained people could even be effective?

Some professionals and pastors still ponder these questions, but most have come to see that trained lay counselors have had a powerful impact both on the church's ministry and on the whole mental health movement. Increasing scientific evidence is showing that laypeople can be competent people-helpers.[4] One writer reviewed forty-two studies that had done careful comparisons of professional and nonprofessional counselors. The nonprofessionals were usually as effective and frequently better than the professional helpers—especially when the counseling concerned specific problems and behaviors.[5] We can only assume that something similar happens when laypeople counsel in the church. Almost no scientific studies of Christian lay counseling have been reported.[6]

WHAT IS LAY COUNSELING?

Counseling involves a caring relationship in which one person tries to help another deal more effectively with the stresses of life.[7] There can be a number of specific counseling goals, but the Christian hopes that counselees will be helped ultimately to cope with pressures, to resolve inner conflicts, to live in accordance with biblical teaching, and to grow as disciples of Jesus Christ and as disciplers of other believers. The process is summarized not so much by the Greek word *noutheteo*, which means to admonish, warn, and rebuke, but by the word *parakaleo*, which means to comfort, support, and encourage, as well as to exhort and admonish.

Counseling was once seen as a foreboding process involving couches, complicated terminology, and foreign-accented therapists with mind-reading skills. These stereotypes are collaps-

73

ing, as they should. Although counseling often involves face-to-face discussion between sensitive, skilled professionals and their paying clients, the term *counseling* means much more. As we have seen, it may include the teaching and learning of social skills, the encouraging of people to join mutual-aid groups, and efforts to reduce personal and community pressures. As defined in this broad way, counseling is a type of caring or people-helping that must involve all compassionate Christians. Of course, there are specialists in this as in all other fields—individuals whose training and expertise enable them to deal skillfully with the in-depth conflicts of those who need special help. But many problems do not need a specialist's involvement. Most can be handled by lay counselors.

Lay counselors are individuals who lack the training, education, experience, and credentials to be professional counselors, but who nevertheless are involved in helping others cope with personal problems. Usually the term *lay counselor* refers to those who have taken at least some training in counseling methods and who volunteer their time and efforts without pay.

Sometimes lay counselors are called *nonprofessionals* or *paraprofessionals*. The words have similar meanings, although *paraprofessional* often is used like *paramedic* to describe competent people who are not doctors but who have been trained for their work. Ward aides in psychiatric hospitals are paraprofessionals.

WHO DOES LAY COUNSELING?

Psychologist Lawrence Crabb, one of the pioneers in this field, has proposed that lay counseling should take place on three levels.[8] Level 1 is counseling by encouragement. All members of the local church should learn to be caring, sensitive people who show support and loving concern for both Christians and nonbelievers.

Level 2, counseling by exhortation, is a more in-depth type of helping. It is done by mature believers who have learned basic counseling skills in a training program.

At level 3, counseling by enlightenment, a few selected Christians in each local church take more advanced training for a six- to twelve-month period. The trainees learn how to handle deeper, more stubborn problems that rarely yield to encouragement or exhortation.

This three-level approach emphasizes the widely held view that all church members should help and care for others, but that only a selected few should be trained as lay counselors. In Romans 12:8, we read that *paraklesis* is a spiritual gift. Such gifts are distributed throughout the body of Christ, as God wills, and are used for the purpose of edifying the church. Not all members of the body have this gift of "coming alongside to help." Those who do should be the people who form the basis of lay counseling programs.

WHO SUPPORTS LAY COUNSELING?

If a program is to succeed, the pastor must show support, encouragement, and a willingness to allow trained laypersons to counsel. Some church leaders appear to be threatened by the lay counseling movement, unwilling to relinquish any of their counseling responsibilities, and perhaps are afraid that lay counselors might be more effective than their pastoral leaders. Others believe that all problems can be resolved by exhortation, and some pastors don't want the local church to give the appearance of being a therapeutic community. Lay counseling programs in these churches are likely to flounder and eventually die. In a recent informal survey of successful lay counseling programs, I found that without exception the pastor was enthusiastic and clearly supportive.

In addition to support from church leaders, three other ingredients are important in any successful lay counseling program: the careful selection of prospective counselors, the effective training of counselors, and the creative use of lay counselors after the training is completed.

HOW ARE LAY COUNSELORS SELECTED?

It is difficult to select participants for lay counselor training.[9] One less than optimistic report stated that training programs tend to "develop out of . . . pressing needs with trainees often recruited in a rather haphazard manner. . . . Usually such procedures involve . . . selection measures which are often of dubious validity and reliability." [10] According to one survey, church selection techniques are no better than secular approaches.[11]

When a lay counseling program is first announced, many people may want to be involved. In one church, the pastor announced the formation of a training class for lay counselors and set up twenty chairs for the first meeting. At the announced time, 140 people appeared—almost half the congregation.

To keep classes small and to be more selective, some churches give training by invitation only. This can create resentment among those who want to participate but are not invited. Some (not all) of these may be people with problems of their own. Perhaps subconsciously, they want help for their own needs, or they hope to hide their struggles by helping others. These people rarely make good counselors.

How, then, do we select the best lay counselors?

First, carefully plan a program for training. This helps you evaluate who might best benefit from the program. If training is rigorous, some people will be dissuaded from participating.

Second, publicly state the importance of caring, but stress that counseling is a gift possessed by only a few believers. Point out that training is required for every person who will be a lay counselor, and indicate that completion of training will not necessarily make one a qualified lay counselor. It is wise to discourage any who want to be involved casually. Although I cannot prove this, it is my impression that some people will drop out if you use the term *caring* instead of *counseling.* The latter word seems more exotic and inclined to attract people who may not be good helpers.

Then announce that there will be a screening process before people can enter the program. This may cause resistance and criticism, but it prevents some insensitive, immature, and otherwise unsuitable people from participating. If you are careful not to "put down" anyone, most people will see the value in initial screening.

It has been shown that criticism is reduced, personal needs are met, and some unsuitable people are screened out if you begin with a class on some general topic, such as "How to Be a Caring Christian" or "How to Find Your Spiritual Gifts." This class could be open to everyone and would be followed later by in-depth counselor training limited to those who had completed the general class and had passed a screening procedure.

The screening might ask applicants to submit a written statement giving a brief personal testimony of personal Christian experience, stating that they agree with the church's doctrinal position, and indicating why they want to be in the lay training program. Applicants might also be asked to come for an interview during which the class teacher or other church leader could try to assess the spiritual maturity, stability, and motivation of the applicant.

If the congregation has access to a trained psychologist, you might want to give a psychological test or two.[12] It can help to find if the applicant is interested in people and willing to make a commitment to a counseling ministry. Ask if others see the applicant as one who counsels effectively. Probably the most effective counselors are those who have been helping people long before any training program was announced.

HOW ARE LAY COUNSELORS TRAINED?

Two important questions are at the basis of any education program: What do trainees need to know? How do they get this knowledge?

What Do Trainees Need to Know?

Professional counselors spend years in school learning the basics of their trade. Some even get their doctorates in the specialized field of counselor education. It will come as no surprise, then, for you to learn that professionals often disagree about what should be taught—and how.

Ideally, a Christian lay counselor training program should include the following:

1. *The development of counselor traits.* A survey of 1,356 teachers and principals found that the ideal nonprofessional is personable, able to relate to others, stable, interested, knowledgeable, and intelligent. Professionals have suggested that

good lay counselors should show empathy, flexibility, good communication skills, genuineness, good judgment, respect for others, and the ability to handle one's own problems.[13]

The best list of people-helper characteristics for Christians is found in Galatians 5. Wouldn't the best counselor be one who shows love, joy, peace, patience, kindness, goodness, faithfulness, gentleness, and self-control? These characteristics are not learned in a counselor training program. They come to those who are committed to Jesus Christ and willing to be molded by the Holy Spirit. A parallel list of characteristics that the believer can "make every effort" to acquire is found in 2 Peter 1:5–8.

Many trainers would agree that there is little value in learning counseling techniques if the counselor does not show a warm, compassionate, sensitive personality.

2. *Basic biblical knowledge.* Christian helpers must be well acquainted with biblical teachings, especially those that relate to personal problems, helping people, the Christian life, and the person and work of the Holy Spirit.

3. *Basic psychology.* It is important to understand how people experience emotions, how they learn and are motivated, how they cope with stress, what causes personal problems, and how we can deal with common issues such as discouragement, anxiety, loneliness, guilt, pressure, or spiritual dryness.

4. *Counseling techniques.* What do counselors do to help others? Training programs must teach counseling skills and give opportunity for students to practice.

5. *Ethics.* Nonprofessionals need to know about ethics and about the dangers in counseling. It also is important to give trainees a thorough knowledge of when and how to make referrals.

The best programs are based on scriptural principles and are aware of established findings from modern psychology. Good training gives students the information they need and helps them gain basic helping skills. Trainees should also be helped to grow personally and spiritually.

All of this may seem overwhelming, but many communities and congregations have access to a competent professional who can "custom design" a program that will meet the church's needs.

In addition, a variety of books and ready-made training programs can give needed information. The appendix lists some available resources for training lay helpers. The books give information; the training programs give both information and guided instruction for small group discussions, use of tapes, and other training exercises.

How Do Trainees Get Their Knowledge and Skills?

Periodically, I receive letters from prospective counselors who are looking for a good correspondence course that will teach them how to counsel.

I doubt that there can be such a course.

Reading books and listening to tapes will give needed information, but counseling is a skill. Like playing the piano, tuning an engine, or performing surgery, good counseling involves both knowledge and practice. It is best if this comes under the supervision of a more experienced counselor. Experts in counselor training agree that knowledge and skill acquisition are both important. Most agree, further, that training should be "sequential"—starting with general instruction that might be open to everyone and moving to deeper levels where the classes are smaller and more selective, the knowledge is more specialized, and the techniques are more sophisticated and difficult to master.[14]

Often training programs include "role plays"—brief periods of practice counseling in which class members divide into pairs, counsel each other about some real or assumed problem, and then discuss the practice counseling with class members who have been observing. Role plays are artificial, of course, but they do give trainees a sense of what counseling is like. They have proven to be valuable training and learning experiences.

It is helpful to divide training into three phases: pretraining, training, and post-training.

The *pretraining phase* involves the selection of materials, announcement of the program, and selection of participants.

If you decide to do an initial course on caring or spiritual gifts, open it to everyone and move on the assumption that there may be self-selection of participants for later courses.

In the *training phase*, there will be opportunities for students to learn by listening to lectures, reading, observing, and practicing skills. Most programs involve at least forty to fifty hours of training, spread over a period of several weeks. It is best to keep the training groups small (twelve to fifteen at most), to meet regularly, to use at least some printed materials, to be flexible, to allow time for students to share their own needs or insecurities, to involve students in role plays, and to discuss complex problem issues, such as depression or homosexuality.

The *post-training phase* is a follow-up time of further learning, discussion of cases, and encouragement. When such post-training is not implemented, lay counseling programs sometimes have difficulty surviving, even though many trainees may continue to apply the training to themselves or informally to others.

A creative program at Elmbrook Church in Wakesha, Wisconsin, illustrates this three-level approach. The program grew out of a need.

The pastor's wife, author Jill Briscoe, was teaching a large women's Bible study which attracted people from all over the Milwaukee area. When the women first began approaching her for counseling help, Mrs. Briscoe referred them to professionals; but she soon concluded that most of the problems did not require such intensive and expensive intervention. Slowly, therefore, a three-year lay counselor training program developed under the guidance of psychologist David Hubbard.

After taking a "Discover Your Spiritual Gifts" class, women either volunteer or are invited to take a counselor training program. Bible study leaders stay alert to find potential class members who are spiritually mature and who appear to have counseling potential.

During the first year of training, these class members meet biweekly for two hours to study doctrine, practice role plays, and share with one another in open, caring fellowship. During the second year, a variation of the "people-helper" program is used (see Appendix), including role plays. Periodically (four or five times each year), an outside resource person will conduct a one-session seminar on a subject such as self-image, alcoholism, or understanding teenage problems. During this second year, a few of the class members are given counselees; but throughout training, students are told that they may not be given counselees even if they complete the training.

At the end of the two years, the "graduates" are available to talk with women who want counseling following the Bible study. The counselors meet weekly with Dr. Hubbard who gives some instruction, but mostly guidance, as cases are discussed confidentially and anonymously.

How Are Lay Counselors Used?

Most trainers have had the experience of carefully selecting potential lay counselors, putting them through a training program, and then not knowing what to do next. The trainees are frustrated because there is nobody to counsel and, sometimes, because the class is over and there is no follow-up. Church leaders may be frustrated because counselees want to see the pastor, preferably the senior pastor, rather than a trained fellow church member. Trainers are frustrated because their hard work appears to have been in vain. This sad situation may not have been anticipated by those who originally launched the program with such enthusiasm.

Nevertheless, the lay counselor can be used in three ways. First, the counselors are helped themselves. Professionals sometimes talk about the "helper-therapy principle"—the belief that the people who get the most from counseling are the counselors.[15] This has been found repeatedly in lay counselor programs. People appear to mature spiritually and psychologically as a result of the training, even though such training may never be used to help others in a formal way.

Helping people informally is a second outgrowth of training. Family members, neighbors, work associates, fellow church members, and others appear to benefit from the informal help given by lay counselors, although it is difficult to determine the extent and effectiveness of such informal helping.

Third, there are more formal church-related programs. Some of these are highly organized; others are not.

One church, for example, broadcasts the morning service and invites listeners to call in to discuss personal or spiritual matters with trained lay counselors who answer the phones on Sunday afternoons.

Another church has a "reach-out" program started by one of the lay counselors. The purpose is to find overburdened mothers in the church or community and to reach out to them with encouragement, practical caring, and counseling help. In other churches, trained lay counselors are used to "reach out" by calling on the sick and shut-ins.

One large church in the South uses trained laypeople to call on nonattending or "disenchanted" members. Working under the direction of the church's professional counseling service, the lay helpers do not attempt to manipulate people back into active church involvement. Instead, the goal is to listen, care, and express willingness to help.

With the increase in church counseling centers, some of the better lay counselors have found a place of service working under the direction of counseling center professionals. Other churches have established counseling services staffed completely by laypersons. In one church, a couple of newspaper articles alerted the community to the availability of free counseling. When people call the church, they are put in contact with the lay counseling coordinator who assigns callers to trained lay counselors from the church.

A more comprehensive approach was developed by Fuller Theological Seminary professor Siang-Yang Tan, when he was on the staff of a church in Montreal. From seven to ten o'clock, two evenings a week, several lay counselors were made available to meet people personally or to talk on the phone. Initially publicized at the church, the service became known to area pastors and church people, some of whom came because they were too embarrassed to approach their own church leaders. A professional counselor always was on duty in case lay counselors had questions or ran into problems that they couldn't handle.[16]

Christian lay counseling is not limited to church settings.

Mission organizations and parachurch groups such as Youth for Christ, Young Life, Navigators, and others have developed their own training programs or used published programs to train staff members and laypersons in counseling skills. At times, the church can work together with these organizations both in training and in lay counseling.

WHAT ARE THE PROBLEMS WITH LAY COUNSELING?

Counseling can be emotionally draining work. It involves helping people in times of crisis and often is time-consuming and schedule disrupting. In launching a lay counseling ministry, several problems can be anticipated.

For example, lay counselor training programs often attract people whose own problems could interfere with effective helping. Included are the *rescuers,* who have a need to control others or to save them from problems; the *pushovers,* who have a serious desire to help, but who are unable to resist the manipulative demands of counselees; and the *superenthusiasts,* who cannot accept rejection or failure, so they are pushy and inclined to quit whenever counselees do not get better quickly. A careful screening and rigorous training program can help to discourage such people from lay counseling involvement.

In many places, there are laws that regulate the licensing of counseling centers. Although these laws often exclude churches or employees of religious organizations, they sometimes restrict use of the term *counseling,* and they may determine who can be sued for malpractice. A highly publicized lawsuit recently charged a pastor with malpractice because of his pastoral counseling. Before you launch a lay counseling ministry, it would be wise to seek competent legal advice about whether laypersons in your area could be sued for malpractice or for harming counselees through the giving of unsound advice and guidance.

Many lay programs are developed by or in cooperation with professionals, but sometimes local professionals resist any form of lay counseling. Some of this resistance may come because professionals feel threatened by the appearance of competition, especially competition that is free of charge. Often, however, professionals have a legitimate concern that well-meaning but minimally trained counselors might do more harm than good.[17] Communication with professionals can help to alleviate these fears and to get support from local counselors who might be able to help with the lay program.

Sometimes problems don't come from professionals outside the church; they come from church leaders, including pastors, who are unwilling to involve lay counselors in the church's ministry. "I'm too busy to make referrals," "I have no time to supervise," "The church members insist on seeing the pastor," or "These issues are too complicated for laypeople" are among the reasons given for not using lay helpers. Each of these has some validity, but each may also be an excuse or mask a desire to retain control of counseling.

On occasion, there also may be passive resistance from the church leaders. Verbally, there is support for the program, but this is never followed up by action. Lay counseling will only be accepted by the congregation when church leaders enthusiastically support the lay counseling program, refer counselees to laypersons, and encourage church members to give and receive help from one another.

In both training and supervision, some instructors are unwilling to permit individual differences in lay counselors. These instructors assume that the approach being taught is the only valid way to counsel. Instructors must be alert to such dangers and try to avoid casting all trainees in the teacher's own image.

Most people are threatened by role plays and often will spend role-play time "getting organized," discussing counseling techniques, or in other ways avoiding the practice sessions. The crucial importance of practical training should be stressed and trainees who refuse to participate should not be permitted to remain in the program.

Some lay counselors complete the training but are unable to handle the drain of counseling others or are unwilling to admit that the load is too heavy. Ongoing supervision of lay counselors, preferably by an experienced professional, can help the counselors both to deal with their own tensions and to withdraw gracefully and without embarrassment if the emotional strain is too great.

Some lay counselors may become overly involved with counselees both personally and, at times, sexually. Post-training supervision can help to prevent this, and so can training programs that emphasize the dangers of intimacy in counseling, the possibility of counselee manipulation, and the importance of referral.

Counselee Supervision

The director of one counseling center recently shared his biggest problem in launching a lay counseling program in the church: "I failed to make enough time available for supervision and follow-up. Training and supervising laypersons has been one of the most exciting and fulfilling ministries that I have ever had, but we can't just train people and turn them loose to influence the lives of others. Lay counselors need guidance."

This comment leads to one problem with lay counseling: a lack of time for supervision and guidance of the counselors. Sometimes it is easier to do counseling ourselves than to find the time and effort to train others, oversee the program, and deal with problems that might arise. This do-it-myself attitude is especially seen in one-pastor churches where there is no staff person who can take responsibility for yet another new ministry.

Several solutions to this problem might be possible. An efficient lay counseling coordinator might be recruited to serve as a "clearing house" person who assigns counselors to counselees and monitors possible problems that can be referred to the pastor or to a lay oversight committee. (People involved in such activities must be able to keep confidences.)

A professional Christian counselor in the community might be hired to supervise lay counselors. This is likely to involve a fee for each session, but sometimes the lay counselors might be willing to absorb such a fee. If no professional is available, do not overlook the possibility of supervision from a psychiatrically alert physician or nurse, a school guidance counselor, or a local vocational guidance counselor. If none of these is available, there can be value in a group of three or four laypersons forming a counseling committee that pools its understanding and gives direction and encouragement to individual lay counselors.

How Do We Work with Professional Nonprofessionals?

When psychologists write about lay counseling, they rarely are thinking of church members. Most lay counseling programs are designed to train students, prisoners, volunteers, and others who can work with their peers.

But what about professionals in the community who are skilled in their own areas of expertise but untrained in counseling skills? These might be called the professional nonprofessionals. Physicians, for example, are men and women professionally trained in medicine, but not in counseling. Lawyers, teachers, law enforcement officers, college and seminary professors, athletic coaches, business people, sociologists, military officers, pastors—each of these has competence and primary training in an area other than counseling. Each is in frequent contact with people who have needs but who may be reluctant to seek help from a professional counselor.

Consider, for example, the senior military officer who once asked how he could help the fighter pilots in his command to deal with the stresses of their work. "They see no need for counseling," the colonel told me over coffee. "But they are under terrific pressure. I want to know how to help them, without giving the impression that I'm trying to play psychiatrist."

There may be similar needs among people in your community. Can the church design training programs that teach believers how to reach out to meet needs in the community?

Such outreach and caring is not only healthy and part of an innovative trend in psychology, it is a biblical requirement commanded by the Lord and taught by the Spirit-inspired biblical writers. They instructed us to reach out in love to help the needy and to bear one another's burdens. Lay counseling in and through the local church is an important move in this direction.

It is a movement that may also help seminary students and other believers put the theology of the Good Samaritan into practice.

CHAPTER FIVE

PREVENTIVE COUNSELING

MAYBE YOU'VE HEARD the story. It's been told often, but I doubt that it ever happened.

It seems that a kind-hearted man was strolling alongside a river one windy day when he heard cries for help from someone who was drowning in the turbulent waters. Heedless of his own safety, the man jumped into the river, pulled out the hapless victim, and began artificial respiration.

Even on lonely beaches, tragedies attract crowds. It wasn't long before a group of onlookers appeared. A few even offered to help, one ran to call an ambulance, and everyone was relieved when the water-logged victim revived.

A few weeks later, it happened again.

Then again.

Soon the whole village was concerned about the many drownings and near-drownings in the river. A lifeguard was hired to rescue the perishing and to call the paramedics whenever there was a cry for help. In time, the local residents built a hospital right on the beach. Rescue teams were trained and outfitted with sophisticated equipment including speedboats and helicopters that could get to the victims with utmost efficiency.

Nobody seemed to notice that the rescue program was costing a lot of money. Everybody agreed that the whole operation was providing jobs; and it didn't seem to matter that some of the people being saved from the water had been pulled out before. Didn't anybody wonder why some of these non-swimmers were rescued, revived, and released, only to be found floundering in the river again?

The community needed a program to teach swimming and to promote water safety. Somebody needed to walk upstream and discover where people were falling into the river—and why. Maybe a firm walkway or a few fences could have been built to prevent victims from losing their footing and sliding into the swirling stream.

But nobody thought like that. As far as I know, the rescue station still exists and does its work day after day.

And people keep falling into the river.

No doubt the moral of this little story is already clear. For many years, we have taken a "downstream approach" to helping.[1] We have waited for people to develop severe problems and then have invested enormous amounts of money and effort into our rescue operations. We have developed sophisticated theories and creative counseling techniques to help pull people through their crises. Then we have sent them back to the same stressful environments that let them slide into their problems in the first place. Is it surprising that many return?

An estimated 15 percent of our population lives at a marginal level of psychological adjustment and could benefit from mental health services. At times, all of us face crises and could use periodic support or guidance from others.

As a giver of this help do you sometimes wonder if the lines of hurting people will ever shorten? Do you find that the same individuals often want to be rescued again and again? Are you surprised that counselors, perhaps like you, have a high rate of burnout? It can be exhausting to work downstream, constantly treating the casualties of a sinful, poorly functioning society.

Jesus said that the poor would always be with us, and the same is true of those who need counseling. We who are followers of the Wonderful Counselor will always be involved in burden bearing and in pulling people through the storms of life. But shouldn't our downstream rescue operations be supplemented by upstream efforts at prevention?

PRINCIPLES OF PREVENTION

The history of medicine shows that no mass disorder has ever been eliminated or controlled simply by treating individual patients or by training new practitioners. Typhoid fever did not disappear until unsanitary conditions were cleaned up. Malaria was not reduced until the disease-carrying mosquitos were controlled. Could it follow that the epidemic of emotional disorders will not be stopped until we develop ways to prevent these disorders from getting started?

Several years ago, the prevention of psychological problems was a "hot topic" that filled the journals and was discussed frequently at conventions. Almost everybody agreed that prevention was important, but nobody knew how to do it. There wasn't much money available for research or for starting creative preventive programs. It was difficult to justify prevention when nobody could prove that prevention worked and when those who needed remedial counseling continued to cry for help and often were willing to pay for professional services. Nobody ever offered to pay for preventive counseling; and few people seemed to want it. It isn't surprising that compassionate professional and pastoral counselors returned to what they knew best: counseling the needy and giving little more than lip service to the need for prevention.

Prevention has two goals: interference and education. Preventive *interference* means that we anticipate problems before they arise and do what we can to keep them from starting. If the problems have already started, the interferer attempts to eliminate them or keep them from getting worse. Returning to our earlier example, interference would try to keep people from slipping into the river. If some had slipped already, there would be attempts to pull them out of the water before they got in deeper.

Preventive *education* means that we teach people how to live, so they can anticipate, cope with, and often avoid overpowering stresses. This is like a water safety program that shows people how to keep their feet on solid ground and how to swim should they ever find themselves in troubled waters.

None of this will be new to Christian counselors. Jesus wanted his followers to live abundant lives, even when they were surrounded by stress (John 10:10). Much of the Bible was written to show how we can resist temptation, mature spiritually, and experience inner psychological stability even though we live in a world filled with corruption, evil, and harmful influences (2 Pet. 1:3, 4). Prevention appears to be at the core of the gospel message.

Types of Prevention

In a book that once was described as "a Bible . . . for the community mental health worker," psychiatrist Gerald Caplan suggested that there could be three types of prevention.[2] The first of these, *primary prevention,* tries to prevent problems from occurring. It teaches people how to avoid pressures, and it often seeks to remove the stressful social conditions that could lead to psychopathology. In medicine, primary prevention programs include those that improve sanitation or innoculate children against disease. The premarital counselor does primary prevention by alerting couples to potential marriage problems and by showing how these problems can be avoided.

Secondary prevention attempts to stop problems that already have started. Not many years ago, whenever a child had scarlet fever, the entire family was quarantined. Aware that the disease was present in the community, public health officials took secondary prevention precautions to insure that the entire neighborhood was not infected. Surgery to remove a beginning cancerous growth is a more recent example. Church marriage-enrichment programs accomplish similar goals when they help couples recognize and get rid of persisting minor irritations that could grow into major marriage-disrupting tensions.

Tertiary prevention helps to rehabilitate people who have had problems and could easily fall back into their old ways. Divorced people, former mental patients, and previous alcoholics, for example, sometimes are criticized or rejected by individuals in the church and community. The stress of this rejection can push people back into the old marital, mental, or drinking problems. Tertiary prevention tries to prevent these relapses.

Prevention may sound easy, but it is difficult to put into practice, especially in psychological and spiritual areas. In medicine, it often is possible to find and then eradicate the cause of a physical disorder. Get rid of the virus and the disease disappears. The same principle applies when a psychiatric disorder is found to have a clear physical cause.[3]

But how do we prevent academic failure, marital breakups, family tension, overwhelming stress in missionaries, burnout in pastors, or spiritual deadness in the congregation? Each of these may have a variety of causes that is hard to identify and even harder to control. Prevention may not be as easy as it first appears.

Goals in Prevention

Several years ago, after her thirteen-year-old daughter was killed by a drunk driver, a determined and grief-stricken California mother founded MADD—Mothers Against Drunk Driving. At first, nobody paid much attention, but soon MADD chapters were springing up all over the country, sister organizations were founded (like SADD—Students Against Drunken Driving), and numerous state legislators passed tougher drunk driving laws.

Why do people get drunk and sometimes drive their cars

into the lives of innocent and sober victims? There are no simple answers, but the question alerts us to some common goals for prevention programs.

First, to prevent problems we should try to *reduce present stress.* Sometimes people drink to "drown their sorrows" or to forget their problems. If they could be taught to anticipate and to cope with stress, such people would have less need to escape into excessive drinking or other self-defeating behavior.

Second, to prevent problems we must try to *reduce the predisposing conditions* that make problems more likely. Prohibition was an extreme effort to stop drunkenness by banning alcohol and closing the bars. This still works well in many Moslem countries. It is hard to get drunk if drinking is socially unacceptable and no alcohol is available.

In contrast, alcohol flows freely in this country. Bars are common, drinking is widely accepted, and alcohol is often glamorized in advertisements. To counter these influences and to remove some of the conditions that encourage excessive drinking, legislators have passed tougher drunk driving laws, raised liquor taxes, and put limits on alcohol advertisements.

For centuries, churches members have been active in trying to change those conditions that breed psychological and social problems. In the past, there were efforts to fight slavery, build hospitals, and change the condition of prisons and asylums. Today, some believers are actively involved in resisting poverty, exposing bigotry, combating racial prejudice, cleaning slums, caring for unwed mothers, helping needy teenagers, and in other ways trying to change stress-producing social conditions.

A different preventive goal is to *strengthen personal resistance* in those who are tempted. Teenagers aren't the only ones affected by peer pressure. Excessive drinkers often succumb because they want to be "one of the boys" and don't know how to resist. Each of us is vulnerable to temptation in some area, and often we don't know how to anticipate and avoid the threats to our marriages, job stability, families, ethical standards, or spiritual lives. Teaching people what to resist and how to say no can be an important part of prevention.

Who Are We Trying to Help?

Some prevention programs try to reach *entire populations.* Everybody in a village is affected when chlorine is put in the water to prevent tooth decay. Many communities could be reached, almost entirely, by television or radio "spots" on practical stress management.[4]

More often, however, preventive efforts are focused on milestone and high-risk populations. *Milestone populations* are those people who are facing major turning points in their lives. It can be stressful to start school, to move into high school, to graduate from college, to change jobs, to move, to get married, or to handle retirement. Each of these transitions can be understood, and people can be helped to anticipate and cope with the stresses involved.

In a similar way, we can work with *high-risk populations*— people who have a high likelihood of developing problems. It is known, for example, that children of alcoholics are more likely to become problem drinkers, that children from divorced homes have less stable marriages, and that people in high-poverty areas are more likely to get involved in crime. Many programs of intervention focus on these high-risk populations.[5]

Before starting any prevention efforts, it is wise to ponder who we are trying to reach and what we are trying to prevent.

Then we can decide whether our programs will be *person centered, family centered,* and/or *society centered.*[6] The first involves working with individuals, couples, or small groups, giving encouragement, warnings, and instructions for dealing with potential problems. The family-centered approaches do something similar with families who are facing the death of a loved one, the breakup of a marriage, the departure of a family member, or some similar disruption in family life. To the extent that the local church is a family of brothers and sisters, it is possible to think of church-wide programs as family centered.

Writings on prevention have tended to emphasize society-centered programs.[7] Usually these involve social action, education, political activities, or the establishment of community outreach programs, such as suicide hot lines or easy-to-reach mental health clinics. Such activities take psychologists out of their offices and church members away from the sanctuary. Society-centered programs cannot be conducted apart from active involvement with the community and the people who live there.

PASTORAL PREVENTION

Has this discussion of prevention taken us a long way from the church and from those Christian leaders who want to be people-helpers? Can our discussion thus far apply to members of the local congregation? Isn't it good enough to notice a problem, guess at its causes, and then forget psychology while we try to do something that will keep the problem from arising again?

That is the way most prevention efforts worked in the past, sometimes with good results. In the nineteenth century, for example, a man named John Snow stopped a cholera epidemic in London by removing the handle from the Broad Street pump. Snow had no idea what caused cholera, but he noticed that people who drew water from one pump got the disease, whereas people who took water from other pumps were not affected. Sometimes we need to take action even though we aren't sure that our efforts will work—or why.

But prevention is more likely to be effective when there is careful planning and awareness of prevention principles. One writer has suggested that the church should carefully develop a "mission to mental health."[8] This would include counselor education for pastors, lay counselor training, development of in-church counseling centers, the providing of emergency counseling services, close cooperation with local mental health centers, and active church participation in community mental health activities. Others have suggested that the church should be involved in mental health education, crisis counseling, the establishment of half-way houses, and the creation of stable environments for former mental patients. Should the church also join community psychologists who are working on behalf of mental health in political, social, economic, and advocacy programs? [9]

All of these efforts can be worthwhile, and no doubt each has attracted the active participation of Christians. It is possible, however, that the church can become so concerned about mental health—important as that is—that we forget our biblical mandate to "make disciples of all nations." Preaching and Christian education can be so overemphasized that believers become theologically bloated—filled with head knowledge but not much interested in healing or in reaching out to the community. It can be equally unbalanced and unbiblical to turn the church into a psychiatric treatment center that tries to meet mental health needs but has no clear presentation of the gospel or no call to discipleship.

PROGRAMS FOR PREVENTION THROUGH THE CHURCH

A recent book attempted to summarize the latest theories and research on preventive psychology, but the church was not even mentioned.[10] Most secular writers fail to recognize that churches have done preventive work for centuries and that they continue to be involved in practical preventive mental health.

Consider the issue of surgery, for example. Research has shown [11] that patients come through their operations with fewer complications, get better faster, and are able to be discharged from the hospital sooner, when they have been told what to expect physically and have been prepared psychologically before the surgery. When patients have caring support from others, hope, confidence, and what has been called a "belief system," [12] many postoperative physical and psychological problems are prevented. Pastors and church members routinely give this kind of pre- and postoperative support. It is unlikely that most of these care-givers have even heard of primary prevention, but their efforts undoubtedly help both patients and families to cope with the stresses of surgery and to avoid potential surgery-related problems.

What else can the church do to prevent problems?

1. *Provide supplies.* According to Gerald Caplan, each of

us needs a continual source of physical, psychosocial, and sociocultural resources or "supplies" if we are to keep from becoming mentally disordered.[13] *Physical supplies* include food, shelter, sensory stimulation, opportunities for exercise, and other influences that maintain health and protect the body from damage. *Psychosocial supplies* include the stimulation that comes from involvement with others in the family, school, workplace, or church. In order to maintain stability, each of us needs to give and receive love, to accept others and be accepted, to not manipulate or be manipulated, to respect others and be respected, to participate in joint decisions, and to be actively involved in mutual activities. *Sociocultural supplies* include the values, customs, perspectives, traditions, and problem-solving skills that come from one's culture. Presumably religious beliefs would be included in this category, or they might be listed separately as *spiritual supplies.*

All of these supplies are available and distributed in abundance through any body of believers that seeks to function in accordance with biblical principles. In stable, nonchanging societies, people know what to expect and tend to have adequate community supplies to help with life's difficulties. In contrast, societies that are in transition—like ours—frequently have shifting values, new ways of looking at things, crumbling traditions, and friendships that are easily broken by moves. This instability shakes the supply source and makes psychological adjustment difficult. In every community, however, there are churches that give stability and point to Christ who is the unchanging "supplier." The old hymn has modern psychological relevance:

On Christ the solid rock I stand,
All other ground is sinking sand.

2. *Give information.* Mental health education (sometimes abbreviated MHE) has become an expanding and effective method of prevention within the counseling professions. Even though it rarely mentions the church, MHE informs the public about mental health issues, tries to remove bias and miscon-

ceptions, gives information about available treatment, calms insecurities, sometimes influences public policy about mental health, and may present self-help suggestions to help people cope with life problems.

Like most other educational approaches, MHE focuses on three issues: the target group to be reached, the program content to be presented, and the educational techniques to be used.[14] The *target group* for any given program may include high-risk or milestone populations, legislators who have the power to bring community change, or teachers and other local care-givers. The *program content* must be accurate, concise, and able to both grab and hold attention. The *educational techniques* in MHE tend to be of two types: lectures, demonstrations, and films that are presented to groups meeting in schools, work settings, churches, or similar settings; and mass media messages that are presented through newspapers, magazines, radio, or television.

In chapter 2, we discussed public counseling as a therapeutic tool. It can also have a preventive impact. Few pastors, at least in Protestant evangelical churches, are likely to plan their sermons as lectures on preventive mental health. Nevertheless, sermons can help parishioners change attitudes about mental illness, get the courage to go for counseling, be more sensitive and willing to care for one another, see the weaknesses in some popular but harmful approaches to personal problems, better understand depression or other common psychological conditions, and to learn practical ways of coping with stress. All of this can have a strong preventive impact on the congregation.

Tucked in my file is a talk on depression that I have given in many churches. It looks at the Old Testament prophet Elijah and draws some modern conclusions about his ancient bout with discouragement.

As I was giving this message in a church one Sunday, I noticed that the organist was crying. After the service, she and her husband told me that two of their sons had died by suicide following depression. The mother herself had been depressed. "But my husband could never understand," she said. "Until this morning!" the husband added that the talk would help him to be more sympathetic and supportive of depressed people in the future.

I have no way of knowing if such a change actually took place. It would seem, however, that every Sunday, in churches all over the world, similar preventive help is reaching congregations through biblical sermons that have implications for mental and spiritual health. Even more powerful, perhaps, are the thousands of adult Sunday school and Christian education classes that can be effective channels for helping people anticipate and cope with the problems of life.[15] To this could be added the special seminars and enrichment programs that are both therapeutic and preventive.

3. *Teach competency skills.* Information, including MHE information, is of limited value if people can't apply it to their lives. A couple, for example, may read books, hear lectures, and watch video tapes on effective communication, but this knowledge isn't helping much if the couple still can't communicate. In addition to knowledge of the facts, people must have the motivation to change and the possession of skills if problems are to be solved and prevented. The competent person has information, drive, realistic goals, and the skills needed to reach goals.

Information, as we have seen, can come through education. Speakers, teachers, and writers can also arouse motivation and help people set realistic goals. But how do people get the skills—especially the "life skills"—that will help them cope with the pressures of living and avoid problems?[16]

Life skills can be divided into several categories, some of which have little to do with the church. *Physical skills,* for example, include athletic abilities, personal health activities, and anything else we do to control or take care of our bodies. *Intellectual skills* enable people to think clearly, learn facts, solve problems, make decisions, and plan for the future. These are skills that most people learn in the home or at school.

Social skills are those that enable us to communicate effectively, avoid interpersonal conflicts, build dating and marriage relationships, be effective parents, and get along with others on the job or in the church and community. Some have maintained that the inability to get along with others is one of the biggest problems facing many churches today. Closely related are *self-management skills.* These enable us to plan and make good use of time, to live in accordance with our values, to set and reach goals, to handle money, to control lust and other self-defeating behavior, to set limits on our mental fantasies, and to maintain a consistent devotional life.

One of the best ways to prevent problems is to help people acquire and use a variety of these life skills. To do this, we must help people see that a given skill is important. Then we teach the knowledge that is required for the skill, model the skill—giving a demonstration of what it looks like—encourage learners to practice the skill while the teacher gives supervision and feedback, emphasize the importance of continued rehearsal, and meet periodically in the future to give encouragement and "checkups" on the new skill.

We do something like this whenever we teach people how to study the Bible or how to share their faith. Golf coaches may take a similar approach when they tutor a novice golfer. Marriage counselors often use this procedure when they teach couples how to communicate. In every case, the learner gets both knowledge and practical experience.

Is any of this the responsibility of a local church? It is if we believe that the church must help people live in harmony with each other (Rom. 12:18), serve and share with one another (Rom. 12:13, Eph. 4:12, Gal. 6:2), set an example for others (1 Tim. 4:12), build better marriages, train children, learn to pray and to grow spiritually, teach others, share the gospel message, and make disciples of all nations. Each of these, and many more teachings of the faith, involve believers in the acquiring and using of skills. When people have these skills, they are better able to deal with problems when they arise. That is the essence of prevention.

4. *Meet personal and spiritual needs.* Many prevention programs are designed to enhance the community and make it a better place to live. It is assumed that this, in turn, will reduce community stress and prevent future problems. The community enhancement approach to prevention is the philosophy that gets many community psychologists out of their

offices and involved in social change, advocacy programs, and local politics.[17] Presumably, there will be fewer problems in the future if we can improve communities now so that individual needs are met and frustrations are reduced. Each church must decide the extent to which the local congregation will be involved in community enhancement efforts.

Remember, too, that the church itself is a community, and activities within the body can contribute to the prevention of problems. Howard Clinebell wrote an entire book to show how growth and healing can both come through the Christian community.[18] The church's message can be "a constructive, creative, healing, life-affirming force," he wrote. It is "a rich source of courage, strength, and growth" for many people.[19]

Freud frequently noted that immature, insensitive, legalistic religion can stifle growth and create problems. But a healthy relationship with Jesus Christ and loving involvement with a compassionate, accepting body of fellow believers can have no equal as an allayer of problems or as a buffer against the pressures of life.

Clinebell suggests that we should look at every part of the church's ministry to ponder how each could stimulate growth, instill mental health, and prevent mental illness. The worship service, for example, can help individuals overcome feelings of isolation, feel a oneness with other human beings, encounter a closeness with God, and find hope, inspiration, challenge, encouragement, and forgiveness. Groups in the church, including Bible study groups, can give acceptance, training, emotional support, inspiration, opportunities for service, support, mutual prayer, knowledge of the Word of God, and what many would see as a simplified form of therapy. Involvement in the church's leadership and administration can give participants a sense of purpose and meaning. Efforts to strengthen family life, teach values, intervene in crises, provide pastoral counseling, and give tangible help to the needy, can each have an influence on prevention, as can the preaching and Sunday school teaching that we discussed earlier.

Clinebell concludes that "a local church works best for mental health when it is true to its mission as a church and not when it attempts to become a mental health agency." "Its rich contribution to mental health" and to the prevention of problems comes because it has vitality and supernatural power. Its members have committed their lives to Christ and should be maturing as "the people of God (a community bound together by a glad commitment to the kingdom which is both among us and yet to be actualized), the fellowship of the Holy Spirit (a ministering family in which the life-renewing Spirit of God can be experienced), and the Body of Christ (his instrument for serving human need in all areas of life)." [20]

A practical example: Do the leaders of your church visit members in their homes? Apparently this was a common practice in the early church and Reformation leaders decided that it should be revived. Calvin emphasized the importance of family visitation and the practice continues to this day in many reformed and other churches.[21]

One church, for example, has divided the congregation into groups, each consisting of several families. The church elders are expected to make periodic and regular visits to each family for the purpose of giving support and encouragement, ministering on an informal basis in each home, exploring areas where help or pastoral care may be needed, and attempting to detect problems before they reach more serious proportions. The visits are not designed to be threatening or unpredictable. Instead, the church elders call first for an appointment, visit informally, and raise several questions when this seems appropriate.

"How are things going spiritually?" the visitors might ask. "What questions or concerns do you have that we might discuss together for a while?" "What is bringing you the greatest joy right now—what is your greatest spiritual difficulty?"

The visits conclude with prayer, and elders continue to pray regularly for each family following the visits. If problem areas are detected, these are discussed confidentially with the pastor or with other church leaders, and follow-up action is taken.

The church takes its family visitation ministry seriously and the pastor is especially enthused. "It seems to me," he wrote, "that family visitation which is carefully planned and sincerely carried out by dedicated undershepherds will be far more valuable than merely that 'ounce of prevention' that we say is better than a 'pound of cure.' " [22]

PROBLEMS IN PREVENTION

It started with careful planning and a lot of enthusiasm. Two respected mental health experts went to a small community in western Canada with a plan to educate the community about mental health. For six months, they showed films, led group discussions, presented their message through the media, and did careful research to see how attitudes were changing.

The experiment was a grand and glorious flop! There were no changes in attitudes toward the mentally ill—at least none that could be measured—but there were a lot of attitudes toward the researchers. Their mental health education program was met with hostility, anger, rejection, and a not-too-polite invitation from the mayor for them to get out of town.

The program was "naively conceived," the researchers concluded in retrospect.[23] They had entered the town without invitation, had not bothered to understand how the people currently felt about mental illness, and had assumed that mental health education and prevention programs could be "dumped" on a passive community. The residents, in turn, were suspicious of these strangers from out of town. There were rumors that the education program was designed to soften public attitudes so that a large and unwanted mental hospital could be built in the community. It isn't surprising that the people resisted.

Prevention is like the weather: everybody talks about it, but not many know what to do about it. Sometimes there is even resistance to preventive counseling—resistance that comes from at least four sources.

Professional resistance. Professionals are by no means united in their enthusiasm about prevention. When there aren't enough qualified lifeguards to pull struggling swimmers from a river, who wants to spend time upstream working with people who have not yet fallen into the water, have no awareness that they might do so, and see no need of help from somebody talking about prevention? Some professionals also may be threatened by the whole prevention movement. Prevention is not good for the therapist's business.

More often, professional resistance comes because counselors simply do not have the time, training, resources, knowledge, or motivation to move into the prevention area. Unlike many physical illnesses where there is a clear cause for a disorder, the roots of psychological and spiritual problems are complex and difficult to identify. If we don't know what causes many disorders, how can we do effective prevention?

Recipient resistance. As the researchers in Canada discovered, people who could benefit from preventive counseling often don't want it. It is not unusual for pastors to find engaged couples who have little interest in premarital counseling. When people are in love and anticipating marriage, they rarely see much need for preventive counseling that is designed to keep their marriage from failing. It is difficult to counsel people who don't yet have a problem and see no need for the counselor's preventive help.

Prevention, therefore, requires considerable tact, creativity, and sensitivity by the counselor. We must respect people enough to let those in the church or community know what we are attempting and why this could be helpful. Try to relate your preventive efforts to the present as well as to the future. Then attempt to get people actively involved; lectures rarely bring permanent change.

Social resistance. Sometimes a whole community will resist your preventive efforts, especially if you are threatening the status quo and cannot produce evidence to show that your preventive programs will, indeed, work. It is difficult to fight racism, poverty, or injustice in the community; it is equally difficult to abolish such attitudes in the church.

A seminary graduate went to a small church several years ago, with a car full of textbooks and class notes on church renewal. Almost immediately, the young pastor began making changes that, he claimed, would revitalize the church, eliminate spiritual deadness, and prevent future problems. As you might have predicted, this insensitive approach created far more problems than it was designed to prevent.

To be effective, prevention approaches have to be gentle.

Church leader resistance. Now that you have read this chapter, how do you feel about prevention? If you are a pastor or other church leader, you may feel that the challenge of prevention is too great and not worth the effort. Like some of your professional colleagues, you may feel that there are so many current needs in your church or community that there is no time to be involved in preventive upstream activities.

Everybody has heard the old adage that an ounce of prevention is worth a pound of cure. This is well established in medicine and a little reflection would suggest that prevention is at the core of much biblical teaching. By giving information, speaking to needs, proclaiming divine truth, and encouraging believers to care for one another, the writers of Scripture have given eternal principles for preventing problems and encouraging both psychological and spiritual growth.

The healing Christian community must be the same—actively involved in both downstream rehabilitation and upstream prevention.

CHAPTER SIX

ENVIRONMENTAL COUNSELING

THE PEOPLE SHOULD HAVE KNOWN it was coming. Mount St. Helen's had been rumbling for years. Scientists had warned that the mountain could "go up" at any time, spewing ashes and raining toxic gases on the helpless communities nearby. The history books told how previous eruptions had resulted in destructive flooding and devastating mudslides.

But that was more than a century ago. Why should anyone panic and run when another hundred years might pass before the mountain would erupt again? Some might have wanted to leave, but they had no place to go. "If you move to California, you worry about earthquakes," one man told a mental health worker. "In the midwest, you worry about tornadoes.

Along the East coast and the Gulf coast, there are hurricanes. And what about the nuclear reactors dotted across the country, not to mention all the seeping toxic waste dumps? Some choice! I'll take my chances with the volcano!" [1]

Some who took their chances died when the mountain finally did erupt. Those who survived saw unbelievable destruction: forests were leveled, rivers and lakes were clogged with mud, crops and wildlife were destroyed, volcanic ash was everywhere. The fishing, lumber, and tourist industries were all in shambles.

Therapists waited for an upsurge in requests for counseling, but it never came. The people cleaned up the mess and went on living. In some families, the tension led to increased child abuse, mate beating, or drinking and drug problems. Most people wondered when tragedy would strike again, but few went for counseling.

"Why go for counseling?" asked one long-time resident. "What could a counselor do?" Nobody can predict when another eruption might occur. Nobody can control a still-threatening volcanic mountain. There is no one to blame for loss of life, property damage, and personal disruption when a mountain does erupt. The people near Mount St. Helen's have to live with the stress.

The residents of Three Mile Island live with a different kind of stress. They had long known that radioactive leaks might be possible, but the nuclear reactor's malfunctioning came suddenly—without warning. There was no earthquake, no storm, no tornado winds, no volcanic eruption. The residents, instead, were forced to flee from something they couldn't see and didn't understand. When they returned to their homes, there was no destruction, no debris to clean up.

But there was fear and anger. Why had this happened? Who was responsible? Why had precautions not been taken? How would the radioactive leak affect their community, lower their property values, influence their health, deform their unborn babies, or shorten their lives? Might another accident occur, venting radioactivity into the atmosphere, contaminating the water, destroying the environment, ruining their health, or maiming their families?

Self-help groups sprang up quickly after the Three Mile Island disaster, but sometimes these only increased anxiety as the group members shared their fears and passed along their latest rumors. Political action groups rushed to bring changes and find government reassurance that things would be better in the future, but these efforts were blocked by impersonal federal bureaucracies and "buck-passing" politicians. Even the scientists couldn't predict how the leak, the dangers, and the stresses would influence people in the future. This was a first-time experience for everyone, including the experts.

The Love Canal disaster was a first-time crisis as well. It came slowly, in the form of seeping toxic chemical wastes and noxious odors. Health problems multiplied in the community, and the value of real estate plummeted. Despite reports of increased chronic illness and numerous birth defects, the Love Canal families were forced to wait impatiently while bitter political battles were fought over who should pay for the damage or reimburse the people for their valueless property.

There were reports of increased depression in the community, anxiety, sleeping difficulties, worries about the coming relocation, marital strain, and parent-child conflicts. There was anger when a well-meaning mental health association distributed a brochure that tried to reassure local residents and give suggestions for coping. The people didn't like the implication that they couldn't handle the stress by themselves.

ECOLOGICAL COUNSELING

How do we help people in the midst of natural or manmade disaster? How can we counsel those who are surrounded by ongoing political or economic stress, uncomfortable living or working conditions, depressing weather, or the continual threat of a volcanic eruption?

Most approaches to counseling make three assumptions.

First, they assume that each counselee is "disturbed," "mentally ill," or in some way needing help. Second, most approaches assume that counseling should find and handle the problems within the counselee. The goal is to help people change so that symptoms are removed or controlled. Third, counselors tend to assume that there is a "normal" environment to which the "abnormal" counselee must adjust.[2]

Often, however, the environment is also unhealthy. Assume, for example, that you counsel an inner-city delinquent about his law-breaking behavior and then send him back home to the neighborhood where his friends are in gangs. Even the finest individual counseling can be undermined when people return to communities, families, or other settings that are filled with conflict, tension, and disrupting living conditions.

The reality of unhealthy environments has led some counselors to adopt an idea from biology. When biologists study *ecology*, they are trying to discover how organisms relate to their surroundings. No cell, plant, or animal stands alone. Each is influenced by the environment, and each can affect the environment in return.

The same is true of our counselees. It is not accurate to view personal problems or mental illness as something entirely within an individual. We cannot conclude that behavior comes solely from a personality trait, a melancholic temperament, a poorly developed ego, a decision to sin, an inner conflict, or a squelching of one's assumed innate potential. We cannot help people effectively if we focus only on inner mental conflicts and ignore the counselee's environment. We are all social creatures. We were not made to be alone (Gen. 2:18). We influence others and are affected in turn by the people with whom we live, work, worship, and play.

Ecological counseling considers both *intra*personal issues that take place within the mind and *inter*personal issues that concern the counselee's relationships with other people and with other things. The sensitive counselor recognizes the importance of both the counselee's inner struggles and the nature of his or her outer environment. To ignore either is to limit our counseling effectiveness.

More controversial, perhaps, is the conclusion that effective counseling must seek to intervene at both levels. Counselors will continue to help people deal with their inner conflicts, worries, attitudes, emotions, thinking, sinful desires, and self-defeating actions. But shouldn't counselors also become more active in trying to change those environments that stimulate unhealthy thoughts, emotions, and behavior?

This appears to be the way Jesus counseled. At times, he met privately with individuals, but he was always aware of social influences. He called for individual commitment but was intent on changing sinful environments. He wasn't a cloistered sage, waiting for the faithful to come seeking help. He was, instead, an active agent of change in his community—a truly ecological counselor.[3]

ENVIRONMENTAL INFLUENCES

Think for a few minutes about the place where you are reading this book. What is the temperature? What is the weather like? What sounds can you hear? Are there distractions nearby? What kinds of furniture surround you? What colors are prominent? Are you wearing comfortable clothes? Are you sitting in a comfortable place? What people are nearby? Do you know them? Do you like these people? What is your inner mood as you read? Do you have worries in the back of your mind? How do you feel physically? Are you tired or do you have a headache? Are you bored with this book? (Surely not!)

Each of these questions helps to describe the environment that surrounds you as you read. Environments keep changing—they never remain completely stable—and, at any time, we can describe environments in different ways.[4]

For example, an environment can be *arousing* or *nonarousing*. When you are aroused, your heart beats quickly, your muscles are tense, and you become alert and ready for action. When the environment leaves you feeling nonaroused, you are relaxed, calm, and sometimes sleepy.

Environments can also be viewed as *pleasant* or *unpleasant*. We feel happy, content, and positive about pleasant environments; unpleasant environments make us feel uncomfortable, unhappy, annoyed, and sometimes fearful.

Environments can also make us feel *dominant* or *submissive*. When we are able to dominate an environment, we feel nonthreatened and in control of the situation. In contrast, some environments make us feel submissive, intimidated, uncomfortable, embarrassed, self-conscious, and not sure how to act.

Have you ever visited a church when you were alone and didn't know anyone? You probably could describe the experience in terms of arousal, pleasure, and dominance. If you enjoyed the people and felt good about the service, you may have left feeling aroused, positive, and with a sense of comfortable well-being. If you were ignored, bored, or disturbed by the pastor's theology, you might have come away feeling differently. A lot depends on the church's environment.

Who is in control? Some psychologists have suggested that people are like puppets on a string—without any freedom to resist or to control environments.

Most of us would disagree with such a viewpoint. We all know of people who experience serenity, joy, and inner peace even while others are "falling apart" because of environmental stresses. Some individuals are able to overlook environmental stresses; others worry. Some believers are able to rest assured that God will protect them; others are less confident.

Before the crucifixion, Jesus assured his disciples that they could know inner peace even in the midst of the environmental trials that were to come (John 14:1, 27). "I am going to send the Holy Spirit to be your counselor," Jesus said (see John 14:26). His coming was intended to bring inner stability that would strengthen the believers as they faced persecution and environmental stress.

ENVIRONMENTAL PSYCHOLOGY

Environmental psychology is the fascinating study of how environments affect us, how we influence environments, and what we can do to cope with environmental stress. Research in this growing field is far from conclusive. Nevertheless, environmental psychologists have made discoveries that can be of practical help to counselors.

Consider, for example, what the design and decoration of

an office might reveal about the person who works there.

Business executives and interior designers are well aware that the size, location, and decor of an office can be an important indicator of the occupant's position and importance. In the corporate world, the more important people have the larger offices, bigger desks, more expensive furnishings, finer carpeting, and best views from their windows. The company president has the most spacious office, sometimes with a massive desk sitting in the middle of the room as an evidence of the boss's power. Down the hall, the lesser executives have smaller offices; the lower a person is in the company heirarchy, the farther is that person's office from the president's inner sanctum. It isn't surprising that some have called this an egotistical "office-psychology game" in which people parade their power and importance by letting others see the environments in which they work. "My office" becomes a status symbol and a way to express position and personality.[5]

It would be easy to conclude that all of this is confined to big corporations that are far from the places where most of us live and work. But our homes (including modest homes), our church buildings, our neighborhoods, other people, the weather, and even the clutter on our desks become part of the environments that affect us—and that we influence.

Inner environments. Have you ever come home from work at the end of a busy day, poured yourself a cup of coffee, and relaxed in an easy chair while you listened to some favorite music? The coffee, the relaxation, and the music all influence the inner environment that is under your skin.

Everybody knows that our feelings, moods, attitudes, and hopes can be influenced by the music we hear, the food we eat, or the rest we get. Fantasies and daydreams influence our inner environments and so do private thoughts about our personal appearance, hairstyles, clothes, or use of cosmetics. Who among us hasn't felt different inside after buying a new wardrobe or changing a hairstyle? When people can make themselves feel better inside, they often can tackle the deeper problems of life more effectively.

Regretfully, there are those who never go deeper than superficial surface issues. These people assume that life meaning and security come to those who are outwardly attractive, able to afford the things that make life comfortable, and surrounded by the trappings of success. Greater affluence and the pursuit of pleasure become the primary goals for these people. Many reach their aspirations and surround themselves with pleasant environments, only to find that their inner lives are miserable and empty.

Physical environments. Tucked between the books in my library is a profusely illustrated volume entitled *The Psychology of the House.*[6] Written by a French architect, the book describes how we express ourselves through our houses and how homes affect our lives.

I once read about a couple who went for marriage counseling because they couldn't decide on furnishings for their home. The husband wanted rooms filled with comfortable and casual furniture that expressed warmth and informality. The wife wanted the house to be a showpiece for her artistic creativity and a way of boasting to their friends that the family was successful enough to own expensive furniture.

The lack of furniture was a source of tension in the marriage, but it also served a useful purpose. By leaving the rooms unfurnished and telling friends that their house wasn't finished, they also escaped from the need to entertain people who might be critical. And they never had to risk failing as hosts.[7]

Our homes can be more than a showpiece of our status or a reflection of our personalities. Interior decorators know that the color of walls, the arrangement of furniture, the amount of light, the presence of plants, and the style of pictures can all affect the degree of arousal, pleasure, and dominance that people feel in homes and apartments. Plants and flowers add warmth and novelty. Brightly lit rooms are more arousing than dim rooms. Chairs that face each other lead to more conversation than long couches that force people to sit alongside one another. "Busy" detailed wallpapers are more arousing than walls painted in pastel colors. Blue, green, purple, red, and yellow—in that order—are most relaxing and most pleasant. Reds and oranges are more arousing than blues and greens. The type and volume of music played can either arouse or calm people in the room.

Some of our counselees live in noisy residences that are filled with tension, clutter, and distracting environmental influences. Is it surprising that they can't relax or find a place to think quietly about their problems? It is hard to "be still" in rooms that are filled with distractions. At times, counselors must help people find places of peace and quiet. In contrast, some counselees need encouragement to brighten their bleak rooms and find places where there is greater stimulation.

Winston Churchill once said that "we shape our buildings, and afterwards our buildings shape us." Environmental psychologists have studied how behavior is shaped by the design of schools, restaurants, offices, hospitals, prisons, theaters, sports arenas, stores, airports, shopping malls, dormitories, and apartment buildings. There is evidence that rates of mortality, fertility, juvenile delinquency, and admission to mental hospitals are all higher among people who live in crowded conditions.[8] Studies of hospitals have shown that patient recovery is faster when there can be privacy and places for friends and family to visit and bring social support.[9] These, and a host of other conclusions,[10] must have influenced the men and women who were appointed to the President's Commission on Mental Health. The somewhat formal language of their final report to President Jimmy Carter has implications for all counselors:

We are firmly convinced . . . that mental health services cannot adequately respond to the needs of the citizens of this country unless those involved in the planning, organization and delivery of those services fully recognize the harmful effect that a variety of social, environmental, physical, psychological and biological factors can have on the ability of individuals to function in society, develop a sense of their own worth and maintain a strong purposeful self-image.[11]

The report proposed that mental health workers must strive to reduce the stressful effects of environmental crises and should seek to understand "the nature of social environments, including those of hospitals and other institutions, so that . . .

115

environments may be created in which people achieve their full potential." [12]

Natural environments. Many years before the president's commission, a medical writer described a different kind of environmental stress. "Everyone is aware of the marked changes in mental state that come with . . . storms," the author wrote. When the pressure falls and the temperature rises, "we are afflicted with a feeling of futility, an inability to reach the usual mental efficiency. . . . Adults on such days are also more quarrelsome and fault finding, with a tendency to a pessimistic viewpoint toward all matters that arise. Such weather provides the most perfect background for marital outbursts of temper." [13]

Do you agree with these conclusions? They may be valid, but they could also be little more than folklore. After decades of research, scientists still have not been able to discover, with certainty, how weather affects us. Most people know about feeling "blue" on rainy days. Crime rates do go up and work efficiency goes down when the weather is hot. Air pollution has been shown to affect health, moods, task performance, and interpersonal relations. When the days are cool and the winds are moderate, students do better work in school and have fewer behavior problems. When the winters are long and dreary, depression is more common and suicide attempts are more frequent. Increased sadness, anxiety, sleepiness, withdrawal, and boredom are part of what psychiatrists call SAD—seasonal affective disorders that come with the increased hours of darkness and the shorter days of winter. When inclement weather keeps families cooped up in confined living quarters, there often is an increase in family violence and marital tension.

The weather affects each of us in different ways. Some people work well when the weather is nice; others are so distracted by the sunshine that their efficiency goes down. When a volcano erupts or a serious storm blows through a community, some "rise to the occasion" and cope admirably. Others collapse emotionally, especially those who have already been under stress and see the natural disaster as a "last straw" in a series of pressures.

No counselor can control the weather, but we can be aware of environmental influences on our counselees and we can help people cope with climate and other environmental stresses.

ENVIRONMENTAL STRESS

Is the moon one of those environmental stresses that disrupts clear thinking and creates mental disorders? The ancients thought so. They spoke of "lunacy," a word that came from the Latin *lunaticus*—"affected by the moon." Hippocrates wrote that lunatics were "seized with terror and fright and madness during the night" because of the influence of Hecate, the moon goddess. In *Othello,* Shakespeare wrote about the "very error of the moon," when it "comes more near the earth than she was wont and makes men mad." [14] Even today, it is widely believed that crime rates, mental hospital admissions, and abnormal behavior are all more common when there is a full moon.

Scientific research isn't nearly as conclusive. The link between deviant behavior and the moon's phases is tentative, at best. Even if it is proven that a link exists, who can say that the moon *causes* the behavior changes? Other explanations might be more likely.[15]

Within recent years, many writers have attempted to explain unusual human behavior in terms of environmental stress. Thousands of scientific articles and hundreds of books have defined, described, analyzed, and proposed theories about stress. Researchers have studied the effects of stress, counselors have helped people deal with stress, self-help seminars have given formulas for coping with stress, and many of us have grown weary of hearing about stress.

But stresses haven't gone away—and they probably won't, as long as environments affect people. Stress, says one definition, "is the process by which environmental events or forces, called stressors, threaten an organism's existence and well-being and by which the organism responds to this threat." [16]

It is possible to look at environmental stress from five perspectives. The counselor can give assistance at each of these.

1. *The stressor.* Environmental stress begins when some

threatening event creates pressure. The event can be sudden, like the eruption of Mount St. Helens; long-term, like the wearing effects of overcrowding or continuing noise; annoying, like the existence of a persisting heat wave; dangerous, like political unrest or a tornado; an occurrence that affects everybody in the community, like the Love Canal seepage; or something more personal, such as the death of a spouse or a fire at home. Sometimes, a feared stressful event does not occur, but the possibility that something might happen creates stress in people who worry.

Three Mile Island is a good example. The nuclear accident was a stress that affected the entire community. It came suddenly, put the people under immediate danger, and demanded a rapid evaculation from the area. After the danger had passed and residents returned to their homes, the stress still persisted. Many wondered if the accident would recur. Media coverage and government hearings about the accident continued to keep anxiety levels high. People worried about reports that the reactor would be restarted, that four hundred thousand gallons of contaminated but "treated accident water" might be released into the river from which they got drinking water, or that explosions and further radiation leaks were still possible.

Like other community residents, counselors can become involved in efforts to insure that environmental stresses—such as overcrowding, aircraft noise, or radiation leaks—are prevented from recurring. When the stress comes from natural events, like the weather or flooding, shouldn't sensitive counselors work with other community residents to prevent excessive destruction in the future? The building of flood gates or higher walls along river banks, for example, could prevent future stress.

While they work in these community activities, Christian counselors also have the responsibility and privilege of prayer, asking God for wisdom and protection as the stresses are encountered.

2. *The evaluation.* Recently, I was staying overnight in a hotel when the fire alarm sounded. I looked out the window

and into the hallway to see if there was smoke, called the front desk to ask if this was a false alarm (they didn't know), and went back to bed.

In the meantime, other guests—including some of my friends—went down the stairs and into the parking lot. Shivering in the cold, they watched as the fire trucks arrived to investigate. One or two of my friends wondered why I hadn't appeared.

The answer was simple. They had assumed that the alarm was to be taken seriously. I had concluded (probably foolishly, even though my conclusion was later found to be correct) that the alarm system was malfunctioning.

People react to stress in different ways, depending on how they view the situation. When a stressor is assumed to be threatening or dangerous, there are feelings of anxiety and a decision to take action. When we conclude that there is no danger, we may react like the colorful old man who refused to budge from his home on Mount St. Helens. Because his name and fiesty personality was the same as former U.S. President Harry Truman, the elderly gentleman attracted a lot of media attention. He told reporters that he didn't think there was any threat.

He died when the volcano erupted.

It is easier to make an evaluation of danger when a stressful situation is familiar, when there is accurate information, and when there is time to think. The people at Three Mile Island had difficulty making decisions about their crisis. The Nuclear Regulatory Commission and the reactor owners gave information that many residents found to be confusing, contradictory, inadequate, and frequently useless. Many people made decisions based on rumor or personal bias. Others denied the danger and convinced themselves, psychologically, that it didn't really exist. Some anxious people tended to panic because their personalities and past experiences had taught them to expect the worst. A few started drinking more heavily so they could avoid facing the stress. Undoubtedly, there were those who turned to their churches and sought spiritual help in dealing with the uncertainties. For many, the stress was especially difficult because they felt out of control. There was nothing the people could do to change their situation.[17]

In any stressful situation, the counselor can help by giving encouragement, providing accurate information, gently challenging unrealistic thinking or denial, and helping counselees reevaluate their perceptions and conclusions. The Christian is also able to help counselees view the stress from the perspective of biblical teaching.

3. *The reaction decision.* When stress is first encountered, the body reacts immediately with increased heart rate, blood pressure, muscle tension, and other familiar physiological responses. Sometimes, especially when there is panic, the mind responds with equal speed and coping action is taken immediately—sometimes with harmful results.

More often, there is time to think about the alternatives. "What can I do in this situation?" a person might wonder. "Are there things that I simply have to ignore or accept?"

Every counselor knows that people rarely are this logical in the midst of intense stress. With little or no conscious reflection, some withdraw from others, refuse to take any action, lash out in anger, try to see the situation in a positive (or negative) light, blame themselves, question the wisdom or existence of God, or find other ways of coping. These reactions depend on how the stress has been evaluated, how stress has been handled in the past, and the extent to which the stressors can be under the person's control.

The counselor has the challenge of helping people decide how to cope. A few might feel guilty about past coping behavior. Others will need guidance in deciding what they can and cannot do next.

4. *The reaction.* Sometimes people decide to take action and then do nothing. Any person who has wanted to go on a diet knows this experience. Deciding what to do is one thing—doing it is something different. There might have been many who decided to move away from Mount St. Helens or from Three Mile Island but never did.

This presents the environmental counselor with another challenge: gently guiding people as they take the coping actions and helping those who decide to act but never do so.

In both cases, there may be guilt, lack of security, and inner struggles.

5. *The after effects.* Sometimes the effects of a stressful situation go on for months or years after the initial crisis has passed. When they have been through trials, few people are "ever the same again." Intense stress influences the faith of those who suffer, sometimes brings bitterness, but often brings greater wisdom, sensitivity, and maturity (James 1:2–4).

After effects are especially powerful when there has been severe stress or when a group of crises have come all at once or in close proximity following each other. People who have had to cope with many problems in the past often find that it is harder to cope in the future. Often there are feelings of helplessness, less ability to think clearly, reduced tolerance for frustration, decreased sensitivity to others, less physical energy, and tendencies to withdraw from others.[18] This is the time when people especially need long-term support, encouragement, understanding, tangible assistance, and prayers from fellow believers who care.

THE CHURCH AS AN ENVIRONMENT

I vividly remember the first time I visited one of my former students. He and his wife had always impressed me with their warmth, and I was struck with this when I entered the front door of their home. The colors, the style and arrangement of furniture, the scatter pillows, the wall decorations—everything silently shouted "welcome!"

People express their personalities in a variety of ways. The clothes they wear, the types of cars they drive, the Christmas cards they send, and the homes in which they live can all show their values, attitudes, and character traits. Even when people have little money and can't afford expensive interior decorators, their homes still reveal much about the residents who live there.

Could the same thing be said about the church?

On a cold December night several years ago, somebody gained access to the church where my family and I worship. Quietly, the intruder poured gasoline around the sanctuary, struck a match, and left. A passing policeman noticed the flames behind the stained glass windows, but the fire had already burned through the roof and was licking the night sky when the first fire truck arrived.

Everybody agreed that we should rebuild (except, perhaps, the person who set the fire), and there was good cooperation between the church members. But the rebuilding raised questions that were far more important than the color of carpet or the size of the new choir loft. What was our purpose for existence? How could a rebuilt building enable us to accomplish our church's goals most effectively? In what ways would the building's design reflect our values and goals as a congregation? Assuming that each congregation has a personality of its own, how would this be reflected in our building? All of these deliberations were colored by a desire to rebuild in accordance with God's will and by our determination to be good stewards of our limited financial resources.

Even before the burned pews were removed from our blackened sanctuary, the pastor began a series of sermons on the purpose of the church. He encouraged us to consider why the New Testament church was created and why it existed. We pondered the unique ministries to which God had called our church. Only then were we in a position to talk about the shape of our new facility.

The early church environment. It is well known that New Testament Christians did not meet in formal church settings. They met in homes, catacombs, and probably in a variety of public places. The setting for worship was created more by the people than by the architecture.

According to Scripture, the early church met for three major reasons: teaching, fellowship, and worship (Acts 2:42–47).[19] The believers gathered to hear the apostles' teaching. There was fellowship around the table as the early Christians ate, prayed, and shared with one another. Worship involved praising God both in each other's homes and in the temple precincts where they met for public worship and public witness. From these early church meetings, the believers went out to turn the world upside down (Acts 17:6).

When people come into your church, what do they see that tells them about God and about his children who worship in your building? Does the position of the pulpit indicate what your congregation believes about the preaching of God's word? Is there a communion table or a baptistry in some prominent place? What is conveyed by the number and color of the windows? Is the room warm and inviting or is the church cold and aloof? Are the people the same?

Even when believers meet in a school or in an old church building constructed in some previous generation, it is wise to remember that the design, shape, and decoration of space can tell much about the church and can influence the activity that takes place there.[20]

The caring church environment. Not far from our rebuilt church, a sister congregation meets in a massive, modern building. Their church has no stained glass windows. There is a stage but no pulpit, tiered rows of theatre-style seats but no pews, room for an orchestra but no prominent organ pipes. The room looks more like a high-school auditorium than a sanctuary for worship.

The church leaders would be quick to state that their ministry is designed to reach community people who wouldn't set foot into more formal looking churches. There are critics of this creative building and its inhabitants, but even the critics agree that the gospel is being preached, that people are coming to Christ, and that believers are growing in spiritual and personal maturity. In a unique way, the building is used for teaching, fellowship, and worship. The church environment is pleasant, spiritually arousing, and not so threatening or dominating that nonbelievers feel intimidated. The church is a superb facility for touching people whom other churches in the community may not be able to reach.

The pages of this book suggest often that pastoral care and counseling cannot be confined to the counselor's office or to the church building. The effective counselor is often found in the community, in close touch with neighborhood needs and concerns.

None of this is meant to imply, however, that the church environment is unimportant. Over the centuries, millions of people have found peace, forgiveness, encouragement, and acceptance within the walls of a local church. Christian leaders have fulfilled the four pastoral functions—healing, sustaining, guiding, and reconciling—within church buildings as well as without.[21] The ministry of the Holy Spirit has never been limited by architecture.

But the Holy Spirit might also work through the design of our church buildings and through our fellow believers who learn, share, worship, and show love within those buildings.

The people near Mount St. Helen's, Three Mile Island, and Love Canal all learned that environment can have a powerful influence on individual lives. This is a lesson that counselors must learn as well. We can shape our buildings and influence our communities, but we must never forget that our communities and the shapes of our buildings can influence and mold our ministries, including our caring and counseling.

CHAPTER SEVEN

BRIEF COUNSELING

THE COLLEGE STUDENT was excited. After several weeks of looking, he finally had found a summer job.

"It's at a camp up north, near the Canadian border," he explained enthusiastically. "And it even involves counseling," he paused, "sort of!"

As part of a program for inner-city teens, the camp that had hired my student apparently teaches reppelling. Each camper is shown how to descend from a steep cliff, using only a rope—and probably a lot of prayer. Some campers love the experience, but others are terrified and need plenty of encouragement.

That was to be the summer job of the student—hanging

on a rope, half-way down a cliff, giving encouragement and advice to stress-stricken campers who were "passing by" on their descent from the cliff top to the solid ground below.

I agreed that this was a counseling job.

Sort of!

Freud would not have agreed. His system of psychoanalysis maintained that effective counseling must involve long-term treatment, provided by therapists who are highly trained, and done with patients who are verbal, introspective, and able to pay. Many professionals who disagree with Freudian theory, nevertheless accept the idea that good counseling is done in an office, on a one-to-one basis, with people who are interested or motivated enough to spend a lot of time discussing their problems. Few counselors have recognized, or admitted, that such approaches may be unrealistic and unworkable with people who are nonverbal or poorly educated. Most professionals have believed—as many still do—that short-term approaches are superficial and ineffective. Would anyone agree that there could be real therapeutic value in words of guidance and encouragement given to a scared inner-city kid dangling from a rope over the edge of a cliff?

We are living in the midst of "a major psychotherapeutic revolution." [1] Self-help programs and mutual-aid groups are becoming more prominent and influential.[2] New therapeutic approaches, some with questionable validity, are appearing with great frequency. Numerous people, even those with little training or competence, are entering the counseling field. And there appears to be a clear trend toward the use of shorter, more widely applied, brief therapies.

THE MEANING OF BRIEF COUNSELING

Brief counseling is sometimes known as "short-term treatment," "brief psychotherapy," "time-limited counseling," "emergency intervention," and similar names. Each involves the use of counseling methods by which the helper deliberately and carefully limits both the goals and the duration of counseling contact.[3] Most brief therapies try to focus on one or two specific problems, deal largely with present crises, spend little time probing into the past, and rarely try to change the counselee's personality. Techniques are flexible, and counselors tend to be active and directive. Although some professionals would consider twenty-five meetings to be "short-term," [4] most approaches schedule far fewer counseling sessions. One writer has even proposed a single-session approach.[5]

WHY DO BRIEF COUNSELING?

I first began to appreciate the importance of brief counseling when I was invited to teach part-time at the U.S. Air Force Chaplain School in Alabama. In all branches of the military, chaplains have discovered that the luxury of long-term counseling is almost impossible. Military personnel are transferred frequently. Many are reluctant to come for counseling, and most want immediate help in the shortest possible time.

We may complain that this reflects the mentality of a nation where people like fast food and quick service. We may believe that lasting change comes slowly. But some people can't or won't wait. They get either the brief help that we are able to provide in a few minutes or sessions, or they get no help at all.

It is probable that most people don't have the time, money, or motivation for long-term therapy, so they get whatever immediate help they need and skip the prolonged counseling. Practitioners may believe in long-term therapy, but research evidence shows that most of their work is short-term.[6] Even Freud slipped. In 1906, he successfully treated Bruno Walter, the famous conductor, in six sessions. Two years later, composer Gustav Mahler was relieved of an impotency problem after a single, four-hour session with Freud—the founder of long-term analysis.[7]

All of this suggests that brief counseling is widely used, largely because it deals with immediate problems and often because it is the only counseling approach for which there is time. Insurance companies may be unwilling to pay for long-term therapy, and many counselees don't want it. Counselors once used the term "dropout" to describe anyone who failed to return after the first session. Now it is recognized that some counselees get all the help they want in a single interview.[8] Numerous approaches to short-term therapy have been proposed,[9] and an increasing body of research is showing that short-term approaches tend to be as valuable as, and often more effective than, traditional long-term counseling.

This should be encouraging to pastoral counselors. Busy and overburdened church leaders rarely have time for long-term counseling—even with those few needy parishioners in every church who seem to be constantly at the door with their chronic personal problems. It is good to know that brief intervention can often make a significant difference, especially with less disturbed people.

There is no evidence that Jesus ever used a long-term approach. Most of his counseling was brief and to the point. It was also effective.

METHODS OF BRIEF COUNSELING

Modern approaches to brief counseling sometimes appear to be in competition with one another. An early leader in the field noticed, however, that "various kinds of short-term psychotherapy in the hands of competent therapists bring about approximately the same proportion of cures." [10] When a counselor is caring, sensitive, skillful, and familiar with short-term counseling methods, people tend to improve, regardless of the methods that are used or the theories that are followed. And in spite of their differences, almost all short-term approaches have some similar characteristics and techniques.

STAGES OF BRIEF COUNSELING

Gerard Egan is a Catholic priest and professor of psychology at Loyola University of Chicago. Several years ago, he developed a "problem-management model" of counseling that has been used to train thousands of counselors, including many Christians.[11]

According to Egan's model, counseling involves three overlapping stages. In *stage 1,* the counselor listens, pays careful attention, asks probing questions, and encourages counselees to "tell their stories." There is an effort to understand the counselee's problems and to get a clear picture of the ways in which these problems have been handled in the past. *Stage 2* involves looking at the problems from different perspectives, exploring new ways by which the problems might be tackled, and setting some problem-solving goals. The counselee is then helped to take action in *stage 3*. A plan of action is discussed, the counselee is encouraged to "try out" new ways for reaching goals, and there is evaluation of the counselee's actions. According to Egan, all of this is based on two core values: respect for the counselee and genuine caring by the counselor.

Egan's system is *not* intended to be a model of brief counseling, but his three stages are similar to the characteristics of many brief approaches. After initial rapport building, counselees are encouraged to "tell their stories" while the counselor listens and tries to understand the core problems. Before long, there is a discussion of counseling goals and consideration of the specific steps by which these goals could be reached. Counselors become teachers, guiding people as they make decisions and encouraging counselees as they actively work on their problem-management activities.

In brief counseling, rapport must be built quickly, counselors must "size up" the problem rapidly rather than making lengthy assessments, counseling goals must be specific, counselors must be active and sometimes directive, and there must be a willingness to try new methods and creative techniques.[12]

In brief counseling, the counselee is assumed to have a pressing problem that needs to be alleviated as quickly and as efficiently as possible. Some professionals complain that this only treats symptoms without handling underlying causes. Brief counselors would reply that people need to be helped with their symptoms and present stresses before they can explore deeper roots of behavior. Brief counseling often leads to more intensive therapy—but not always.

Who benefits? It should not be assumed that brief counseling benefits everybody. Short-term approaches rarely help people who are psychotic, deeply depressed, excessively withdrawn, addicted to alcohol or other drugs, involved in entangling sinful behavior, or victimized by physiologically based mental disorders.

Research shows that brief techniques are best suited to people whose problems came somewhat suddenly, to those whose previous adjustment has been good, to people who know how to relate well to others, and to counselees who are highly motivated to solve their problems.[13] Brief techniques have been used successfully with suicidal persons,[14] but people who are excessively dependent, consistently angry, and highly anxious are better candidates for longer forms of counseling.

Techniques of Brief Counseling

It is sobering to realize that right now, as you read this book, some woman is probably being raped, a helpless child is being beaten by his or her parents, a spouse is being battered by a mate, a drunk is inflicting pain on another person, or someone is being victimized by criminals. We read about these things in the papers but have grown to treat them so casually that we rarely are shocked and often forget that these are real people in the midst of life-altering crises. A pastor may see some of these people in emergency rooms or in their homes, but few professional counselors are on the scene after such traumas occur.

That has been changing with the development of "emergency psychology." This is a difficult, sometimes dangerous type of work that is done by courageous and sensitive counselors who have special training for dealing with crisis situations. Usually the work is done in cooperation with local police departments and community agencies. Emergency counselors rarely sit in comfortable offices waiting for counselees to come seeking therapy. Instead, these professionals respond to telephone calls for help. They go immediately to the scene of emergency, try to reduce tension or diffuse anger, and often give practical suggestions for dealing with an immediate crisis. Known technically as "strategic therapeutic intervention," this is brief counseling in its most dramatic form.[15] It is the kind of situation that pastors periodically encounter but rarely enjoy.

Under less traumatic conditions, brief counseling can be satisfying and even enjoyable. Its techniques are focused on two major issues.

Clarifying the problem. According to one writer the sensitive counselor has five initial goals in brief counseling.[16] He or she must create hope, often when people have lost hope; demonstrate understanding of the counselee's emotional state; identify the major problems in living that are of immediate concern to the counselee; formulate some mutually acceptable goals for counseling; and decide on a time limit for attaining these goals. The brief counselor keeps an eye on the clock but avoids any appearance of impatience, rushing, or worry about time. If counselees ramble to seemingly irrelevant topics, the counselor gently pulls the discussion back to the main issues being considered.

Stimulating change. When there is agreement on the goals for counseling, the counselor then seeks to help the counselee change in ways that will reach these goals. The best brief counselors are familiar with a number of ways by which people can change.

1. People change by learning new behaviors. Often the brief counselor will ask a counselee to describe how a problem has been managed in the past. One woman, for example, told how she talked frequently to her husband but complained because he never listened when she spoke. At the counselor's suggestion, the woman gave an example of her way of talking to the husband. With this understanding, the counselor was able to make suggestions for a better approach to communication. Then the counselor modeled that approach and encouraged the woman to follow the counselor's example.

Brief counseling often involves role play. At first, everybody feels awkward and uncomfortable about this, but the learning-modeling-practice approach has been very effective in helping people change their behaviors.

2. People change by gaining new skills. Many times, people have problems because they don't know how to study, hold a job, get along with others, interact with family members, assert themselves graciously, communicate, relax, or handle stress. Each of these is a skill; each has to be learned.

Recent, innovative approaches to counseling have emphasized that skill training is an important part of the counselor's work. Once again, there must be an understanding of the skills that are needed, some instruction and modeling in skill development, and opportunity for practice.

3. People change by learning to think differently. Every counselor knows that a person's thoughts have a great influence on how one feels and acts. It is difficult to handle the problems of life if a person thinks, "I am no good. I am incompetent. God doesn't care much for people like me."

Diet counselors have noticed, for example, that people who feel embarrassed about their obesity often have a very low self-concept. As they lose the weight, these people often gain self-assurance and interact more confidently with others.

Within recent years, "cognitive psychologies" have risen to prominence and popularity among counselors. These approaches help people see their problems differently, get rid of self-destructive and irrational beliefs, get a clearer and more realistic perspective on their life situations, and eliminate unrealistic thinking. The counselor may gently challenge the counselee's ideas or more strongly attempt to persuade a counselee to think differently. Once again, the counselor becomes an instructor who teaches and models new ways of thinking.

Pastoral counselors, of course, have used these approaches for many years. When people hear biblical teaching or are challenged about their unhealthy and sinful behavior, there often are changes in thinking.

4. People change by practice. Even when people think differently, however, they sometimes do not act differently. Sometimes they don't know how to act, or they may be too shy to practice what they are learning in counseling.

This has led a number of counselors to give tasks or homework assignments that are carried on apart from the counseling session. One of my former professors has called this "instigative therapy." [17] The counseling session instigates tasks that are to be practiced as the counselee goes about his or her weekly activities.

Tasks are designed to be realistic—not like New Year's resolutions that are too many, too complicated, too difficult, and, thus, unlikely to be accomplished. The tasks remind the counselee that real change comes away from the counseling session.

This reduces dependency on the counselor and gives people practical experience in self-management and in personal coping. The woman with the communication problem was given realistic techniques for talking with her husband and was instructed to practice these at home, one at a time.

After the counselee has practiced his or her new skills, there is a follow-up evaluation with the counselor. If the counselee has been unable to complete a task or homework assignment, the reasons for this are discussed, and new (sometimes more realistic) tasks are planned.

Perhaps you have noticed that this is similar to the "reality therapy" that William Glasser proposed many years ago. Some professionals criticized the approach with its emphasis on present problems (instead of focusing on the past), its deemphasis on the unconscious, its goal of teaching people how to live, and its recognition that morally responsible behavior is important. It is not surprising that many Christian counselors were impressed with the reality therapy method that once was described as "a new approach to psychiatry." [18] It is a new approach that has contemporary relevance to brief counseling.

SINGLE SESSION COUNSELING

Hidden within the pages of an old photo album is a picture of me, dressed as a gangly teenager and talking to the pastor of my church. I must have been about seventeen at the time, but I still can remember the topic of our conversation. I had been struggling with career decisions and wanted the pastor's advice about college. Our discussion took place in the public dining room of an old campground (one of my friends took the picture), and we probably didn't talk for ten minutes. But so far as I can recall, this one pastoral counseling experience did more than anything else to set the direction of my future vocation.

My experience as a short-term counselee is not unique. An increasing body of research [19] has confirmed what psychiatrist Lewis R. Wolberg wrote over two decades ago: "Human warmth and feelings, experienced by a patient in *one session* with an empathic therapist, may achieve more profound alterations than years with a probing, detached therapist intent on wearing out resistance." [20]

To be of maximum effectiveness, single-session counseling should involve more than giving "human warmth and feelings." The counselor should have specific goals and techniques that can be used within the single interview. Psychologist Bernard L. Bloom has listed twelve guidelines that can apply equally well to short-term, long-term, and pastoral counseling.[21]

1. *Identify a focal problem.* This involves listening carefully and raising a few questions that enable you to identify "one salient and relevant issue" that will be the focus of the counseling. Try to state this in a few words:

"Your main concern is deciding where to go to college."

"You won't be able to decide what to do about marriage until you do something about the feeling that you are such a terrible person."

"It looks like you're going to have to forgive your father."

2. *Do not underestimate the counselee's strengths.* You will only be involved with the problem for a short time, so you have to count on the counselee's ability to cope after the counseling is over. Part of your goal is to encourage the counselee to use his or her strengths and abilities more effectively. It may be wise to remind yourself and the counselee that *with God*, all things are possible (Matt. 19:26).

3. *Be prudently active.* Try to ask questions and to give information when needed, but avoid lectures, preaching, a lot of advice giving, and stories about yourself (these can be distracting). If possible, use the counselee's language, but first be sure that you know what the key words and phrases mean. Don't use complicated words or wander from the central problem issue.

4. *Present your interpretations tentatively.* It is easy to jump to conclusions quickly, but your jumps might lead you to incorrect decisions, especially if you have not been listening carefully. For this reason, it is recommended that interpretations be presented tentatively: "I wonder if . . . ," "Have you ever thought that . . . ?" If a counselee rejects your suggested interpretations, your conclusions may indeed be wrong, but re-

member that your observations might also be correct.

5. *Encourage the expression of feelings.* Let people know that it is okay to cry or to express anger. Jesus expressed feelings and it is artificial and inaccurate to pretend either that we have no emotions or that emotional expression indicates weakness. Sometimes, you may have to point out discrepancies: "You're laughing, but there's nothing funny to laugh about." Dr. Bloom's experience led to the conclusion that there is "no more effective technique than explicit and accurate recognition of the feelings the client is carrying around."

6. *Use the interview to start the problem-solving process.* Help the counselee see that something must be done and discuss how this could be accomplished. Often this will mean that the counselee gets involved with some other person. "Could your father shed some light on that?" you might ask. "Why don't you tell your wife how insecure you feel?"

These suggestions let the counseling continue after the interview is over. Sometimes it is helpful to call a few days later to inquire gently if clients have followed through. If I am talking to someone after a public address, I will often encourage the person to "write and tell me what happens." This can help with motivation.

7. *Keep track of the time.* No counselee likes to feel rushed, so the counselor must keep an awareness of time. Try to pace yourself so there is time for exploration and clarification of the problem, identification of goals and problem-solving actions, and gradual closing of the interviews.

8. *Do not be overly ambitious.* It is tempting to try to accomplish too much. More effective are approaches that focus on one issue. When you attempt too much, counselees can get so overwhelmed that they don't make any changes.

9. *Keep factual questions to a minimum.* Ask only what you need to ask. Sometimes "demographic information" about one's family, birthplace, occupation, or interests is of no real value in the counseling.

10. *Do not be overly concerned about the precipitating event.* Sometimes a crisis or past event precipitated the counselee's request for help, but this may not be important when the interview begins. More important is to know what the

counselee needs now. You can find out by asking a basic question. "What can I do to be helpful?" Usually this will get the counselee talking.

11. *Avoid detours.* At the beginning, you will have to let the interview go into a variety of directions while you focus on the main problem. Once you have selected a topic for concentration, try to avoid distracting discussions.

12. *Do not overestimate what counselees know about themselves.* Even highly educated or sophisticated people can be oblivious to things about themselves that are obvious to others. Have you ever had a counselee shout that he is not angry or tearfully tell you that he is not sad? It can be helpful to know about the counselee's self-awareness and to point out what the counselee doesn't see.

13. *Other considerations.* In addition to the above suggestions, the Christian counselor remembers that we are dependent on God for wisdom and on his Holy Spirit to give insight and sensitivity. It is wise to seek divine guidance before we see the counselee, to pray silently during the interview, to raise spiritual issues when this seems relevant, and to maintain an attitude of humility.

Writing a short, concise sentence or letter is harder than composing lengthy, rambling prose. In the same way, it is harder to help people effectively through a single interview than to engage in long-term counseling. Our short-term goals must be more limited, and our time must be used more effectively.

I doubt that my pastor knew much about this when he counseled me as a teenager. He was effective because of his concern and determination to help. You can be even more helpful in counseling if you keep the preceding brief counseling principles in mind.

BRIEF COUNSELING AND THE CHURCH

Counselors don't like to think about this, but research evidence shows that untreated people sometimes get better as quickly as those who are counseled.[22] Does this mean that counseling doesn't do any good or that most people would recover spontaneously whether they get counseling or not?

Not necessarily. When no counseling is available, it appears that most people turn to the "natural environment" for help. Relatives, friends, neighbors, fellow workers, and other community people become continuous and readily available sources of help. When they cannot (or are reluctant to) get specialized help from a professional or pastoral counselor, many people get informal and spontaneous treatment from nonprofessionals in their environments.

Brief counseling recognizes and encourages reliance on this network of natural helpers. Friends may not give the specialized help that could come from a professional, but friends are available and often willing to give sympathy and advice. Even when problems are being discussed with a professional, the counseling is of limited value if new learning cannot be applied outside of the counselor's office. Involvement with friends and others can give opportunity for the counselee to practice new skills and can prevent an unhealthy dependence on the counselor.

This has significant relevance to the church. Brief counseling by a church leader can be more permanent and effective when it is supported by members of the congregation who show encouragement and caring concern.

Sometimes, the counselee feels that there is no support in the church or any place else. Often these counselees are people whose arrogance, demands, or complaining attitudes have alienated them from friends, family, and congregational sources of help. Such distressed people need help in learning how to relate to others, just as members of the church and family may need guidance in knowing how to encourage, accept, and help people who tend to be social misfits. If we are to follow the example of Jesus, church members should specialize in helping social misfits—especially when they are believers (Gal. 6:10).

SPECIAL FORMS OF BRIEF COUNSELING

Brief counseling can be used in a variety of situations, but there are times when it is clearly the treatment of choice. Examples include telephone counseling, suicide counseling, and crisis counseling.

137

Telephone Counseling

The telephone is available to almost everyone. It is familiar, easy to use, and inexpensive (unless the call is long distance.) The telephone caller can remain anonymous and has the freedom to hang up at any time. It is much less threatening to call a telephone hotline than to visit a counselor, and the telephone is available day and night. Callers don't have to worry about appearance, dress, lifestyle, or other social and physical barriers that might interfere with counseling. Also, counselors can often be reached without an appointment.

Nobody knows, for certain, how many telephone counseling services are available. Hospital emergency rooms, poison information centers, paramedics, police dispatchers, and fire departments can always be reached by phone when emergency help is needed. Some media talk shows encourage listeners to call and share their opinions or vent their emotions on the air. Religious television programs often give callers a number to dial for counseling. Many people call to hear recorded "dial a prayer" messages, and others use the telephone to get recorded information from hospitals, counseling centers, or colleges.

Typical of many programs is a telephone service developed by a southern university. Each fall, a brochure is distributed, listing a variety of student problems: what to do when you are failing; how to know if you are pregnant; how to cope with stress; handling financial problems; how to know if you are becoming an alcoholic; symptoms of venereal disease; and others. Callers can dial a number and hear a brief recorded message on these or any other problem that they choose. At the end of the recording, callers are invited to stay on the line if they would like to talk further with one of the volunteer counselors who are available twenty-four hours a day. Many students call several times and listen to the messages before they can muster the courage to talk to a telephone counselor.

In literally hundreds of telephone hot-line centers around the country, trained volunteers give advice, encouragement, information, support, prayer, and referral help to thousands of callers every day. By being available and by listening, telephone counselors meet the needs of innumerable suffering strangers. Lonely people find temporary friendships at the other end of the telephone lines. Depressed people often find hope. Drug users and alcoholics can find a source of practical help. The "weak and heavy laden" can find the spiritual rest, refreshment, and peace that comes from a relationship with Jesus Christ.

One review, published several years ago, estimated that over ten million people are served by telephone counseling every year. "The hotline makes help, information, advice, comfort, and counseling available around the clock," the reviewers wrote. Telephone counseling "transcends geographical barriers where seconds can make a life or death difference and offers an acceptable form of help to many persons who would not ordinarily come into a helping agency." This specialized form of brief counseling has become what the reviewers called "the fastest growing helping service in the country." [23]

Should your church be involved in this kind of ministry? It is expensive and time consuming to train counselors and find staff for a round-the-clock telephone counseling service. Even when the telephones are answered by unpaid volunteers, there is a need for professionals who can give "back up" help in emergencies. Many calls come late at night or on holidays, such as Christmas, when it is difficult to find volunteers to handle the phones.

But churches can provide brief telephone counseling on a more limited basis. Earlier we mentioned a church that has volunteer counselors available for only a part of Sunday afternoon, following the weekly telecast of the morning service. Another church advertises that counselors are available for two evenings each week. And in every church, members can be encouraged to call shut-ins and others who are in need. There can be no more accessible vehicle for brief counseling than the common telephone.[24]

Suicide Counseling

For most people, attempted suicide represents the final step on a journey that began weeks, months, or even years before.[25]

The suicidal person is often depressed, angry, lonely, without hope, and overwhelmed by feelings of helplessness. As a last resort, these people often turn to suicide prevention centers and telephone hotlines. Eventually, many will be involved with long-term therapy, but at the time of the suicidal crisis, there is a need for immediate brief counseling from a sensitive, caring, skilled helper.

Suicidal people often talk to friends, relatives, or fellow believers who have little or no training in suicide prevention. Friends probably have prevented thousands of suicides by listening, caring, giving encouragement, and getting the suicidal person to more qualified help. In suicide prevention, we should never underestimate the importance of friends within support systems who care enough to get involved.

Trained suicide counselors, including the volunteers who answer phones, often are able to evaluate a suicide threat within a few minutes. By careful listening and use of occasional questions, knowledgeable counselors can often determine the cause and severity of the crisis, can assess the degree of risk, and can reach conclusions about the counselee's ability to cope. As with other forms of brief counseling, the helper is often directive and active in giving guidance, making suggestions, getting emergency medical help to people who have already swallowed pills, and sometimes arranging for hospitalization or other removal from an especially threatening environment. Frequently, it is necessary to offer hope, to help people deal with feelings of anger or depression, to give practical guidance for handling the present crisis, and to arrange referrals.

Few churches have formal suicide prevention ministries, although many church members work in secular centers. Even without church centers, most pastors at some time are faced with counselees who threaten suicide. There is no standard way to handle such situations except to pray silently (and often audibly), to be compassionate and caring, to make use of your counseling skills, and to share the hope that comes to those who are in Christ. Criticism, impatience, insensitivity, or any indication that "good Christians don't consider suicide" can each undermine your helpfulness. Remember that suicidal cries for help almost always mean that more serious problems are present. These can be dealt with in depth at a later time. The counselor's immediate task is to prevent the suicide and to help the counselee cope with the present crisis. This is a specialized form of brief counseling that often is done effectively by church leaders.[26]

Crisis Counseling

No pastor needs to be told that church leaders are also involved with crises. All of us face crises at times and many of us turn first to the pastor for help. Some writers make a technical distinction between crisis intervention and brief counseling,[27] but both attempt to help people cope with stress and handle life problems within a short period of time.

Experienced crisis counselors are involved in several overlapping tasks. First, there is *problem deliniation* when the counselor listens and tries to determine the most basic and pressing counselee need. Then comes *evaluation,* an attempt to determine the severity of the crisis as it affects the counselee, an assessment of his or her strengths, and an effort to find what environmental support might be available in the social system. *Contracting,* the next task, is a brief discussion with the counselee of the goals that counseling will try to reach.

Intervention comes throughout the counseling but is especially prominent after the first three stages are complete. The crisis counselor listens, encourages the counselee to talk, helps him or her identify friends who could help, sometimes confronts, provides factual information, discusses various coping approaches, gives advice or suggestions, talks about the help that comes from God, and often gives homework assignments. After the intensity of the crisis begins to pass, the counseling moves to the *termination* stage, followed at some time later by a telephone call or personal visit for *follow-up.*[28]

While a pastor is often called to provide this kind of brief help, it sometimes is forgotten that many people turn instead to the police. Some estimate, depending on the community, that between 50 and 90 percent of calls to police departments involve family crises, domestic violence, serious assaults, and other complaints of a personal or interpersonal nature. Men and women, who were expecting careers in crime control and law enforcement, find instead that they are round-the-clock community crisis counselors who too often are injured or killed in the line of duty, as they attempt to handle interpersonal conflict. Within recent years, courses in crisis intervention, conflict management, and brief counseling have become an important part of police training. Such training is most effective if it includes consideration of the emotional strain and personal burnout that this kind of work heaps on police officers and their families.

On the day when I was planning to complete this chapter, I received a brochure in my mailbox, announcing publication of a new international journal of short-term counseling. The brochure told of "remarkable breakthroughs in short-term psychotherapy," reported that there had been a rapid increase in recent research dealing with short-term approaches, and expressed "exciting new possibilities" for brief counseling.

Professionals now see value in short-term approaches that are similar to what church leaders (and policemen) have been doing for years. Brief counseling can be much more sophisticated, but it is no more important than the work of that former student who spent his summer dangling from a rope, encouraging inner-city teenagers who were afraid to scale a cliff.

CHAPTER EIGHT

CROSS-CULTURAL COUNSELING

"I CAN'T BELIEVE *you're* here!" The young man from our church youth group was genuinely surprised to see me at a rock concert. I was surprised myself.

For several years, my teenage daughters had tried to convince me that every father needs to experience a rock concert at full volume. I agreed to go but felt more than a little self-conscious. Among the thousands of jumping excited teenagers who filled the chairs and bleachers, there appeared to be no more than two or three other people of my age. And I wondered why *they* were there.

I tried not to be analytical, but my mind drifted back to a previous conversation with a retired violinist who had spent his life as a classical musician. "Contemporary music is the music of our culture," he had told me. "Rock music is an expression of the youth culture. Some of the lyrics are bad, of course, and many musicians lead blatantly immoral lives. But if you look beyond that, a rock concert is one of the best ways to understand the culture of modern young people." The Christian rock concert that I attended was giving me a good observation point for seeing a large segment of contemporary Christian kids.

Many of us learned about culture in high school or college anthropology courses, but we rarely think about such issues in our day-to-day work. Counseling textbooks say little about cultural differences, and even when we realize that immigrants or members of minority groups come from different backgrounds, this seldom affects our counseling ministries. Most of us give little thought to the idea that we too are part of a culture. Even within the congregation, there are people from a variety of cultures—including the youth culture that prefers rock music instead of the great old hymns of the faith that the choir likes to sing.

WHY BOTHER WITH CROSS-CULTURAL COUNSELING?

Cross-cultural counseling has become a "hot topic" within the past several years. Books, articles, seminars, courses, and workshops all point to the conclusion that counselors must give more attention to cultural issues.

"Counseling and psychotherapy have failed with respect to the culturally different," writes Derald Sue in his excellent book on cross-cultural counseling. When counselors fail to heed cultural differences, Dr. Sue continues, they may "restrict rather than enhance the well-being and development of the culturally different." Even though they don't mean to do so, counselors show prejudice and discrimination when they assume that all of us belong to the same culture.[1]

Looking at Other Cultures

Everyone knows that overseas travel has become increasingly popular within recent years. Students, business persons, and tourists by the thousands have been criss-crossing the oceans and invading each other's countries. More than one hundred thousand professional missionaries live in foreign countries and bear the name *Christian.* Large numbers of short-term missionaries, pastors, volunteer workers, and "tent-makers" [2] serve abroad in a variety of settings. In the United States alone, over two hundred fifty thousand students have come from other countries to live and study in North America.[3]

When they first arrive in another country, visitors often feel excited, fatigued, and sometimes overwhelmed by the new and unfamiliar. Far away from family and friends, they are immediately forced to cope with different currency, different expectations, different customs, and sometimes a different language.

If they stay for any length of time, foreign visitors often go through a five-stage personal reaction cycle.[4] Often this is seen in visitors from abroad, but you might also have noticed this in yourself if you have visited other countries. First, there is *enthusiastic acceptance* of the new culture. Everything is new and exciting. The visitor feels enthusiasm, euphoria, and warmth toward the people. This feeling may last for as long as two or three weeks.

Soon there are feelings of *doubt and reservation.* The newness begins to fade, and the visitor recognizes that things are not as rosy as they first seemed. The absence of familiar food is annoying. It is frustrating to be faced perpetually with people who speak a language or have ways of thinking that are different from one's own. The strain of adjustment begins to wear us down.

Perhaps it is not surprising that a period of *resentment and criticism* often follows. "It is at this stage that foreign students tend to find their professors incompetent, their dormitory rooms inadequate, their course work misrepresented, and their colleagues antagonistic. Businessmen tend to find the hotels inefficient, the barbers backward, the railroad stations mislocated, and the airplanes dilapidated." [5] Military people living in other countries become critical of their "backward" hosts. Missionaries find it is easier to criticize than to share Christ's love with a people and culture whose ways seem so unusual.

Residents of the host country may have difficulty in being patient with the criticisms that come from their visitors. Recently, I drove for two hours to meet some people who had come here to study. They had been in the country for about a month, and they started complaining from the moment we met. They griped about the United States in general and the part of the country where I live in particular. It was difficult to keep calm and hospitable. I wanted to state bluntly that if they didn't like it here, they were free to leave—the sooner the better!

In time, most visitors move to the period of *adjustment,* when they begin to see that unhappiness and critical attitudes are due to the difficulties of adjusting to the unfamiliar. There comes a time for more objective observation of the new situation, and soon there is movement to the stage of *accommodation and evaluation.* Here the visitor acquires a degree of comfort in the new culture, finds nationals who become friends, and actually begins to enjoy the experience.

Almost all of us go through these stages when we make prolonged visits to other parts of the world. Even when we move to another state or neighborhood there can be similar adjustments. These adjustments will be easier if there are friends in the new location who can give encouragement, guidance, and understanding. When pastoral counselors are aware of the adjustment process, they often give better help to the visitors or new residents who are recent arrivals in the community.

Looking at Our Own Culture

Have you ever heard of a culturally encapsulated counselor? The term was proposed several years ago to describe counselors who overlook cultural variations in their counselees and who assume that everybody can be counseled in the same way.[6]

Most approaches to counseling have been developed by well-educated white therapists, working mostly with well-

educated white counselees who accept the values and attitudes of a well-educated white culture. Our views of right
and wrong, pathology, money, the ideal family, the importance of success, the influence of early childhood, or the best
ways to counsel, all reflect the accepted opinions of our culture. Even our preferences in music, our views of Christian
maturity, and our opinions about the ideal worship experience
are reflections of our culture. It is not surprising, therefore,
that almost all forms of modern Western counseling are encapsulated in white, Western, educated-class, cultural values.[7] It
should not come as a surprise for us to discover that traditional
counseling approaches often fail to fit other cultures—including minority subcultures within our own communities or congregations.

In a two-day workshop on cross-cultural counseling, I was
startled to hear a speaker begin with the bold assumption that
all counseling is cross-cultural. Each of us brings our values,
perspectives, beliefs, and expectations to the counseling session, and communication is likely to be more difficult if the
counselor and counselee bring different cultural viewpoints.[8]

This is illustrated in the following diagram: [9]

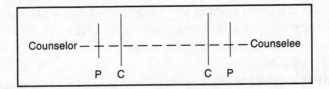

For communication to be effective, the counselor and counselee must get through two kinds of barriers. The personal
barriers (P) refer to the values, attitudes, and perspectives
that are held by the individuals who are communicating. The
cultural values (C) refer to the values, ideas, and viewpoints
that are accepted by most people in the culture. Communication will be easier and counseling can be smoother if the counselee and counselor have similar personal perspectives (P) and
come from the same culture (C). The greater the differences
between the personal and cultural perspectives, the greater
the potential communication difficulties.

Assume, for example, that an older female counselor, who has been raised in English-speaking North America, talks with a young male student counselee who has been raised in the Orient. The two cultures (C) may have different views on women as counselors or on the appropriate attitudes that a younger person should show to someone who is older. In addition, this counselor and student bring their personal (P) perspectives about counseling, aging, and sex roles. These differences may never be mentioned, but they are present and influencial regardless of whatever problems might be the reason for the counseling.

Western white culture. The word *culture* was first used by educated Europeans who presumed that they were more enlightened, more civilized, more aware of advances in medicine and technology, more politically sophisticated, more wealthy, more refined—i.e., more "cultured"—than the ignorant, lowly, "uncultured" peasants who did not appreciate or understand the finer things of life. Early in this century, anthropologists began using the word *culture* in a different way: to describe the customs, beliefs, values, and behaviors that characterize a group of people.[10] This assumes that everybody is part of a culture—even counselors, educated wealthy people, and those who are known as "uncultured peasants."

Several writers have attempted to describe white Western culture.[11] It has been noted, for example, that white Westerners have distinctive:

• attitudes toward time—we adhere to rigid time schedules, disapprove of wasting time, and are very much controlled by the clock;

• personal habits—we make direct eye contact, rarely hug, tend to control our emotions, wash our hands frequently, almost never spit in public, shower every day, eat with utensils instead of our fingers, and rarely have animals in the house, except for a cat or dog;

• views of the family—we value youth rather than family elders, emphasize the nuclear family rather than the extended family of numerous relatives, tend to be informal at home, and are open in expressing our feelings to family members; and

• perspectives on individual achievement—we believe in rugged individualism, assume that people should take responsibility for their own lives, emphasize the importance of education and the drive for success, value autonomy, and reward those who are assertive and hard working.

Most of us assume that English is the best language, that science is the most effective way to gain knowledge about the natural world, that democracy (as we define it) is the best form of government, that people develop best when they have freedom from government and other external controls, that free enterprise is the superior system of economics, and that counselees can get better if they are determined to do so. We tend to believe that our culture is the most advanced, the most correct, and the most Christian.

Christian culture. Believers are not only a part of the culture in which we live, but in addition, each of us is part of a religious culture.

Consider, for example, the contemporary evangelical church. The members believe that the Bible is the Word of God and that there is only one way to become a Christian (through confession of sins, recognition that Jesus Christ died to pay for our sins, belief in the Lordship of Christ, and submission to his authority). Often there are accepted beliefs about the proper method of baptism, the preferred version of the Scriptures, the ideal lifestyle for committed believers, the best types of music and worship, the acceptable form of church government, the major mission of the church, and even the biblically correct form of counseling. When other believers present different conclusions on these and similar issues, there can be misunderstanding and miscommunication.

If we are to be effective counselors, it is important that each of us understands something about the values, beliefs, attitudes, and cultural perspectives that we bring to the counseling session.

PREPARING FOR CROSS-CULTURAL COUNSELING

When we begin to recognize the influence of our own culture, we are better able to appreciate and understand the cultures of those with whom we counsel.

On one of my trips to Central America, I had a long conversation with a friend who was honest enough to share his views about missionaries. "Many are good, but at least half of them should stay home," he stated bluntly. "They huddle together in their own little compounds, speak the same language, keep their own customs, sometimes maintain a 'know-it-all' attitude of smug superiority, and don't try to understand my people." Perhaps my friend was overly critical, but he was a pastor and his views no doubt expressed the opinions of other believers in his congregation and culture.

Communication, including communication of the gospel and of counseling help, is likely to be ineffective unless the communicator attempts to understand the culture that he or she wants to reach. The missionary's goal should be biculturalism, the ability to move freely between two cultures without the need to frequently "get back to my own kind of people." [12] Those of us who serve at home have the difficult but important task of understanding the values, typical behaviors, perspectives, and emotions of our counselees' cultures. This involves understanding people who come from different countries or have different color skin. It also means understanding the subcultures of those who are elderly, teenagers, single adults, atheists, strict in their religious beliefs, obese, homosexual, suspicious of counselors, depressed, or unemployed.

Cross-Cultural Understanding

Have you ever wished that Jesus and some of the New Testament writers had been more organized in their manner of teaching? Why didn't they give three or four clear points in each of their messages, deal with one topic completely before moving on to the next, and avoid the use of so many confusing parables?

Such questions reflect our educated, Western way of thinking. An African student once challenged me to change my writing style so I could communicate more effectively with his culture. "Don't give organized lectures with points and subpoints," he said. "Tell stories instead. My people learn best when they hear parables."

A counseling professor from Nigeria has echoed the same

message. He wrote that Nigerian students often experience intense culture shock when they come to study in America. African superstitions, parables, myths, and supernatural explanations are dismissed in the West as being irrelevant and primitive. There are few familiar rituals, almost no group supports, hardly any interest in Africa, and little understanding of the African student's view of life. When this person goes for counseling, he or she finds that counselees in America are expected to share intimate problems with a stranger, discuss ambiguous issues like "self-concept" or "adjustment," work on issues independently rather than submitting to the direction of a respected authority, and solve problems without the support and help of family members. Nondirective counseling is confusing to a student who comes from a culture where healing is authoritative and directive. The admission of problems (especially to a white, foreign counselor) is embarrassing to a student who has learned that stresses should be shared only with family members or a close friend. Counselors are rarely helpful until they understand these Nigerian perspectives.[13] Similar paragraphs could be written about Asian Americans,[14] Puerto Ricans,[15] American Indians,[16] and a host of other cultural groups.

How do we gain understanding of a counselee's culture? First, there must be a sincere desire and effort to learn. On a speaking trip to Australia, I discovered that one member of the local committee had not wanted me to come. When I met the man in Sydney, I gently raised the issue and asked why he had opposed my visit.

"I'm tired of North Americans who come here with all their pat answers," he replied abruptly. "You people never take the time to understand our culture or to read about our way of life." He went on to describe a couple of books that every visitor to Australia should read and suggested that if I had really wanted to communicate, I would have taken the time to read these books.

Imagine his surprise when I reached into my briefcase, pulled out the books that he mentioned, and showed how I had underlined and attempted to digest their contents. The man who was my critic became one of my most enthusiastic supporters because he knew that I was serious in my desire to understand his culture.

Reading can be a helpful way to learn. In addition to what we might find in the local library, counselees can also suggest helpful books or articles. If you expect to be overseas, ask missionaries to suggest reading material. Whenever I am invited to speak to a group that is culturally different, I ask for suggestions about reading material that will help me to understand. Counselors can do the same.

Counselors can also listen and ask questions. None of us can be experts on a variety of cultures or subcultures. We have to ask nonthreatening questions and learn from the counselee whatever is socially appropriate and expected. This understanding is crucial if we hope to intervene and give help.

I once had an Oriental student who was highly anxious about the prospects of failing, even though she was getting excellent grades. Telling her to relax and to stop worrying would have done no good. It was more important for me to talk with her about the Eastern importance of "saving face" and about ways to keep from "losing face" while she studied within an educational system that was very different from what she had been used to at home.

Overcoming Cross-Cultural Barriers

Tim Stafford is a writer whose monthly column in *Campus Life* magazine is read eagerly by thousands of teenagers. When he and his wife went to Nairobi, Kenya, to develop a youth magazine, they took a wealth of publishing experience and had high expectations for starting a first-rate publication.

It wasn't as easy as they expected. Almost immediately they were confronted with barriers of language, time perception, different values, and anti-Westernism. Even though they were working with fellow believers, the Staffords found unfamiliar attitudes towards colonialism, work, socializing, economics, and interpersonal relations. How easy, and refreshing, it would have been to withdraw into friendships with fellow missionaries and other Westerners. How difficult it was for them to persist in breaking through international barriers.[17]

Even when cross-cultural counseling takes place in our own

communities, there are a number of barriers that must be overcome. Most noticeable, perhaps, are *language barriers.* It is difficult to communicate with people whose native language is not English. Often, it isn't much easier to talk with those who use ghetto expressions, teen talk, frequent swearing, or other expressions that you normally do not use and may not understand. Words are often accompanied by gestures and other forms of nonverbal communication that may be unfamiliar. The sooner you learn what the counselee means (you may have to ask) the better will be your communication and rapport.

Prejudice can be another barrier. Simply defined, prejudice is a prejudgment that may be built more on rumor and expectations than on fact. We each carry our own values and opinions into counseling. We tend to assume that our ways are the right ways.

Tim Stafford went to Africa with the idea that efficiency is more important than spending time with people. The Africans had different priorities—and the Western missionary had to adjust. Mrs. Stafford, who worked as a counselor, had to put aside her biases quickly.

Another barrier can be the counselor's *pride.* It is easy to assume that we are being noble, condescending, and solicitous when we counsel with someone of another culture. If we even think such thoughts, counselees pick them up almost immediately and "turn us off." A Latin-American friend commented on this succinctly. "We're not stupid. When somebody looks down on us, we spot it right away. We may be polite— that is part of our culture—but we have no respect for the person with superior attitudes, and we pay no attention to what he or she says." Counselors must remember that we are in no way innately superior to those whom we try to help.

An additional barrier is *anxiety.* Often we don't know what to say, how to act appropriately, or how to help without being offensive. Stafford reached an interesting conclusion about this feeling of anxiety and uncertainty. "Some missionaries seemed naturally friendly, flexible, patient. Mixing came easily to them. . . . they won appreciation because it was clear they meant well. I saw, in contrast, others who, having studied anthropology and communication principles, could give lectures on African culture; but they did not know how to get along." [18] Knowledge of another's culture is important. Love and respect for others, as persons, is crucial if one is to counsel effectively.

Building Trust

Counseling has been described as "a sociopolitical act." [19] In America, especially, the majority white citizens have most of the power, wealth, status, influence, and education. Members of minority groups sometimes see white counselors as enemies, manipulators, critics, or money grabbers. The counselor has to overcome these biases and help counselees feel confident and trusting.

Trust can be built in several ways. The absence of any notions of superiority and the showing of genuine interest in the counselee both help. When the counselor is seen as being well-informed, capable, intelligent, proficient, and caring, there is also a breakdown of mistrust. Trustworthy counselors are also sincere, respectful of other cultures, open, and clearly lacking in any desire to oppress or get personal gain from the counselee. When the counselee and counselor are both believers, many other barriers fade and trust frequently is more immediate. [20]

DOING CROSS-CULTURAL COUNSELING

The conversion of the Ethiopian eunuch is a well-known event in early church history. In the midst of a busy and successful ministry, the apostle Philip was directed to leave everything and travel to a lonely stretch of desert road where he met an important official who was the royal treasurer for Queen Candace of Ethiopia.

Philip noticed that the man was reading the Scriptures as he rode in his chariot. "Do you understand what you are reading?" Philip asked. The subsequent conversation led to the Ethiopian's conversion and baptism.

Could this be considered an example of cross-cultural counseling? Philip and the Ethiopian came from different countries and had different backgrounds. But one man clearly had a problem and the other helped.

Notice that Philip was sensitive to the Holy Spirit's leading, was available to help, was flexible enough to move away from his more familiar methods, went to the Ethiopian (instead of waiting until he came for counsel), offered assistance, listened to the man's problem (the traveler didn't understand what he was reading), shared with him in a somewhat directive manner, followed the verbal session with action (the man was baptized), and withdrew to allow the queen's treasurer to go on his way rejoicing (Acts 8:26–39).

Even before the counseling began, Philip recognized the need for divine guidance. With this awareness and supernatural help, the evangelist was able to cross cultural barriers, use flexible approaches, and intervene successfully in the Ethiopian's life.

Cross-Cultural Counseling Effectiveness

Experienced counselors know that there can be no "how-to-do-it" formulas for counseling. Each counselee is unique. Each counseling situation is different from all others. Each person must be helped in an original way. Rigid counselors are ineffective counselors.

In spite of this, there are counseling principles that apply to most cross-cultural situations.[21] Cross-cultural counseling is most effective when the following are present:

1. The counselor shares or understands the counselee's *world view.* The counselor does not need to accept and agree with the counselee's perspectives, values, beliefs, and attitudes. But the effective counselor attempts to see the world as the counselee sees it. This involves more than intellectual understanding. The effective cross-cultural counselor tries to imagine the counselee's world emotionally—as he or she feels it.

Culturally skilled counselors possess specific knowledge about the counselee's ethnic, race, or cultural group. This means being familiar with prejudices that counselees might encounter. The effective cross-cultural counselor is "aware of the history, experiences, cultural values, and life-styles of various racial/ethnic groups." [22]

The more we know about any one cultural group, and the more we know about many groups, the more we are likely to be effective as helpers. The culturally skilled counselor is one who continues to explore and learn about other groups. This continual learning may be easier for the Christian counselor who has an interest in missions and a desire for in-depth learning about other societies.

2. The counselor is *sensitive to his or her own cultural perspectives* or values and acutely aware of the uniquenesses of other cultures. Instead of cultural snobbery, there is a belief that other cultures, while different, are not innately inferior.

3. The counselor is *comfortable with differences* that do exist in terms of race, beliefs, expectations, social backgrounds, and attitudes. There is no feeling of awkwardness because the counselee is different.

4. The counselor seeks to understand and use culturally appropriate *communication skills*. The counselor must be able to send and receive both verbal and nonverbal messages accurately and appropriately.[23] This means that the counselor must understand the counselee's language, gestures, and slang expressions. It is important to understand what counselee's think about direct eye contact (many cultural groups avoid this), tone of voice, rate of speech, talking about intimate issues, physical contact such as hugging, answering questions, the appropriate distance between people when they talk, use of titles, and other issues that may be different from the counselor's expectations. If you don't understand some of these issues, it is fine to ask on occasion, but ask sparingly. Some cultures perceive such questions as a mark of incompetence.

5. The counselor is flexible and sensitive to cultural differences in the use of *counseling skills*. According to Sue, "Studies have consistently revealed that (a) economically and educationally disadvantaged clients may not be oriented toward 'talk therapy'; (b) self-disclosure may be incompatible with cultural values of Asian Americans, Chicanos, and Native

Americans; (c) the sociopolitical atmosphere may dictate against self-disclosure; (d) the ambiguous nature of counseling may be antagonistic to life values of the minority client; and (e) many minority clients prefer an active/directive approach to an inactive/nondirective one in counseling." [24]

These conclusions about minority counselees apply with equal validity when the counselor is part of the minority, counseling in another culture. In each case, there must be a flexibility of approach that integrates the counselor's knowledge and techniques of counseling with the counselee's needs, problems, and cultural uniqueness.

When Philip successfully counseled that Ethiopian eunuch, it is probable that neither of them knew much about cross-cultural communication. But the world was simpler then and life may have been less stressful. Nevertheless, the same Holy Spirit who guided Philip can also direct us—especially if there is an awareness of cultural differences and a complete acceptance of the fact that God has allowed each of us to be culturally unique and different from all others.

SPECIAL ISSUES IN CROSS-CULTURAL COUNSELING

Half a century ago, a European psychologist named Kurt Lewin proposed a "person-environment" approach to understanding human behavior. People, said Lewin, do not exist in isolation. Each person is part of an environment, and each environment includes people. As the following diagram shows, the person influences the environment and the environment, in turn, affects the person.[25] The effective counselor under-

stands and attempts to bring change both in the environment and in the person.

Most Western therapies emphasize change in persons.

These therapies help persons: (1) understand themselves better; (2) get a clearer and more accurate understanding of the environment in which they live; and (3) change their perceptions, behaviors, and attitudes so they can fit into the culture better.

Even in the West, however, environments also may need to be changed. Psychoanalyist Erich Fromm once wrote a book in which he argued that our whole society is insane and in need of radical transformation.[26] The Christian counselor (who probably would disagree with many of Fromm's humanistic conclusions) agrees that society is sick and in need of change. Individuals sometimes need help in changing their environments and in finding social systems that give support in times of stress.[27]

Coping with Cross-Cultural Stress

Stress, as we have seen, affects individuals in different ways. Events or frustrations that you or I might take for granted could be major stresses for visitors or for people who are members of minority groups.

I once lived in Switzerland for almost a year while I did research for a book. My knowledge of French is passable, but I still can remember the frustrations of trying to get a license plate in Geneva. The Swiss applicants seemed to be having no problems, but I had a variety of difficulties in filling out the forms, getting the car inspected, and answering the examiner's questions. I felt isolated, helpless, and stupid. I didn't understand the bureaucratic procedures and felt incompetent in my use of French. There were no Swiss friends there to give me support, guidance, or encouragement. I had the self-conscious feeling that everyone was noticing me as a foreigner.

Do foreigners and minority residents feel something similar in my community? Do they feel rejected, incompetent, not sure how to act, confused, embarrassed, lonely, and overwhelmed by the unfamiliar? If so, how would they respond if I appeared to offer counseling—in a language that they didn't completely understand, expecting them to reveal their intimate frustrations, without the presence and support of their relatives, and in my psychologist office? By putting ourselves into the place of our counselees, we can often understand their insecurities more easily.

The counselor must try to find some common ground for communication. There must be an effort to understand how counselees view the environment and how they see themselves as persons in the environment. It helps if we can learn what counselees would like to see changed. What might be their goals for counseling? Can we share with them how counselors work and then cooperate in solving problems, instead of imposing our rigid approaches and goals on to them? Can we show compassion, let them know that we understand, and involve familiar support systems? Can we help them find the hope that comes through faith in Jesus Christ and involvement with a caring body of believers? These questions get to the essence of cross-cultural counseling with those who struggle to cope with stress.

The Issue of Values

A number of psychologists and others have argued that many people today seem to have no values, no beliefs, or no standards that they hold with conviction. Because of this, many have no ethical guidelines, no religious perspectives, and often no real reason for living.[28] Christian counselors respect each person's right to make value decisions without pressure or manipulation. At the same time, we are aware of the value vacuum in many counselees and are willing to share biblical values freely and tactfully.

The cross-cultural counselor must use special care, gentleness, and sensitivity in sharing values. Members of minority groups often are anxious to please. Many feel intimidated by the more powerful counselor. In order to keep peace, some counselees will overtly agree with the counselor's values or religious beliefs even though there is no clear understanding or desire to believe something new.

Christian counselors have a different challenge when their counselees do have firmly held values, but values that the counselor cannot accept. What does the counselor do, for example, if the counselee wants to bring in the local witch doctor or occult reader to help in the counseling? Some psychological writers have suggested that "native healers" can be effective partners with the counselor in bringing change and solutions to the problems of minority counselees. The Christian realizes that such alliances may be of temporary benefit, but ultimately they will be destructive to the well-being of the counselee. That may have to be stated gently and firmly, but if you do so, consider other modifications in your counseling that could fit with the counselee's values.

As an example, suppose you are dealing with a male counselee whose values are different from yours.[29]

He lives for the present; you believe in planning for the future.

He has little concern about punctuality and doesn't think much about the clock; you are very time conscious.

He sees no value in education; you have several degrees and value formal schooling.

He is generous, gives things away, and owns almost nothing; you are concerned with acquiring possessions and making financial plans for the future.

He had great respect for the wisdom of old age; you are more youth-oriented.

He freely cooperates with everyone; you are honest enough to admit that you tend to be competitive.

He rarely makes decisions without consulting the family; you believe in individual responsibility and decision making.

He isn't very religious but is willing to accept all religions, including spiritism; you are a committed believer.

He doesn't much trust white people; you are white.

Can you counsel with such a person? Clearly, you can't change some of your important values, and you won't give up your biblical convictions. But surely you could work within the counselee's views on age, time, competition, generosity, or education. Could you be flexible enough to allow some family members to be present when you counsel? You might not agree with all of the counselee's viewpoints, but perhaps some aren't important enough to challenge.

What is important is your willingness to recognize, understand, and respect cultural differences in counseling.[30]

Is this the approach that Paul took? He was a Jew, called

to preach the gospel to the Gentiles. His letters often took the form of counseling with believers in churches scattered throughout the Middle East. In many respects, therefore, Paul was a cross-cultural counselor.

"Though I am free and belong to no man," he wrote to the Corinthians,

I make myself a slave to everyone, to win as many as possible. To the Jews I became like a Jew, to win the Jews. To those under the law I became like one under the law (though I myself am not under the law), so as to win those under the law. To those not having the law I became like one not having the law (though I am not free from God's law but am under Christ's law), so as to win those not having the law. To the weak I became weak, to win the weak. I have become all things to all men so that by all possible means I might save some. I do all this for the sake of the gospel, that I might share in its blessings (1 Cor. 9:19–23).

Without in any way compromising his beliefs, Paul was flexible enough to recognize and reach across cultural differences so he could help and win some.

Can there be any finer example of cross-cultural helping?

CHAPTER NINE

PLANNING COUNSELING

HE HAD SPENT the night in the street, curled between a concrete trash receptacle and a newspaper vending machine, across from Rittenhouse Square in Philadelphia. His only possessions were the dirty plaid blanket that was pulled around his head like a shawl and the clothes that had hung on his emaciated frame for as long as he could remember—baggy corduroy pants, ragged shoes, a faded wool skull cap, and a well-worn shirt. He had no income, no one who knew his name—Crawford—and no place to wash or find shelter from the cutting November winds.

For three years, he had slept in the streets or tried to find a little warmth in public buildings or abandoned houses. Often, his toilet was a public alley; his food came from garbage pails or from sympathetic passersby who would give him a stale donut or a container of coffee. Sometimes, people also passed him a dollar or two, but most ignored him—too preoccupied or embarrassed to even glance at the old man who shuffled along the streets or sat for hours on the sidewalks, propped against cold brick buildings.

Occasionally, somebody would swear at him. Once, a few drunken sports fans had celebrated their team's victory by tossing him over their heads like a rag doll. Another time, he said, a well-dressed dog walker had urged his Doberman pinscher to urinate on the old man. But after dark, the streets would become deserted, and Crawford would settle down for the night, often talking out loud to the only person who had listened all day—himself.

This is not the story of an alcoholic or a Skid Row derelict, too lazy to work. Crawford was, instead, the victim of a well-intended, highly publicized, expensive government program that didn't work.

For many years, mental hospitals had been filled with backward people who existed, sometimes for decades, in despicable inhumane conditions. Many of these inmates had been locked away, abandoned by their families, largely ignored by professional counselors, cared for by overworked and underpaid hospital employees, supported by the taxpayers, and given up by society with little hope of release or recovery.

Then came the invention of psychotherapeutic drugs. Almost overnight, anxious, hallucinating, agitated, and violent people calmed down. Previously withdrawn psychotics began to communicate and reestablish contact with reality. Deeply depressed individuals began to see hope. Psychiatrists and other professionals were amazed at the changes and began to think about discharging some of their patients. Government leaders talked about closing expensive mental hospitals, clearing the back wards, and reintroducing people to society.

In a moving and powerful message to Congress, President John F. Kennedy proclaimed that the nation had neglected its mentally ill for too long. We must "stimulate improvements in the level of care given the mentally disabled in our state and private institutions, and reorient those programs to a community centered approach," the president urged. The time had come, "to reduce, over a number of years, and by hundreds of thousands, the persons confined to these institutions. . . . To retain in and return to the community the mentally ill and mentally retarded, and there to restore and revitalize their lives." [1]

Thousands of people were released from their wards and many found jobs. Laws were passed, insuring that mentally ill persons would not be confined to hospitals unless there was "clear and present danger" to themselves or others. The back wards did close, and large mental institutions were boarded up or refurbished as office buildings and condominiums.

But thousands of people, mostly chronic schizophrenics, couldn't cope very well with life outside the hospital. Crawford was one of these ill-fated people, wandering in the streets like an abandoned puppy, until he was found by a sensitive reporter from the *Philadelphia Inquirer.* In a series of powerful articles, the newspaper told Crawford's story and enabled him to find lodging in a Veteran's Administration hospital.[2] Others, probably more than a million, have not been so fortunate.

How do we respond to stories like this? How do we react to reports of runaway kids, teenage prostitution, gang violence, increasing alcoholism, drug use in the high schools, or hunger and incredible poverty in our land of affluence? Sometimes we are made to feel guilty because of our lack of practical involvement and presumed insensitivity. Often we feel powerless—but also a little relieved because we are too far away to do anything of value.

Jesus never expected one person to deal with all the world's problems. He ministered to the needy people with whom he came into contact and expected his followers to do the same. He advocated no complicated social or counseling programs; but he did instruct us to be concerned about the needy, and he warned that it is foolish to begin a project without prior planning and cost accounting.

How, then, can churches most effectively minister to the

needs of hurting people in their own congregations and communities?

BUILDING A COUNSELING PLAN

Leaders in the early church maintained a healthy balance between the *planning* done by people and the *leading* that came from the Lord.

Philip, as we have seen, planned his ministry as he moved from village to village in Samaria, but he was willing to be led into the desert where he met the Ethiopian eunuch (Acts 8). Peter planned his work in reaching the Jewish nation for Christ, but he was willing to obey when the Lord led him to the home of a Gentile named Cornelius (Acts 9). Paul planned his missionary trips and hoped to visit Spain, but he eagerly obeyed when he got the unexpected leading to take the gospel to Macedonia (Acts 16).

In a modern and complex society, it is logical and wise to plan our ministries carefully. No one church, or one pastor, can minister to everybody. Few churches have the resources or calling to be full-service institutions that do all things for all people. Each local body is unique, composed of individuals with different gifts, ministries, and burdens. Each congregation must decide, "What are the specific callings and unique ministries for our church?" Who are the people with the greatest needs in your community, and how can you and your church be equipped to help? All of this involves careful planning by the people.[3]

But planning must always be subject to leading from the Lord. It is possible to construct man-made plans, to pursue these with enthusiasm, and to give little or no serious thought to what God might want us to do. To avoid the dangers of planning "by merely human means," one church has established guidelines for developing new ministries: [4]

• We will not undertake anything without a clear sense of the Holy Spirit's direction, confirmed by eldership.
• We will not utilize any means of promotion or fund raising that depends on human genius or style to be effective.

• We will not pursue anything that overlooks the priorities of *worship, relationship,* and *ministry.*

At the same time:

• We *will* pray much, often, and always.
• We *will* think—trusting God's Spirit to give clarity, coherence, and conviction to us all.
• We *will* believe, knowing that "without faith it is impossible to please God" (Heb. 11:6).

The church's perspective is summarized by the pastor's paraphrase of Philippians 3:13–14: "Brethren, I do not count myself as having attained any goal, but I do this one thing: leaving what is past, I reach ardently for what is ahead—in quest of that goal which is God's high calling to Christlikeness."

How can we call people to Christlikeness, help those who are in need of counseling, bear the burdens of those who are weak, and insure that the local body of believers functions effectively as people-helpers? How can we most effectively "prepare God's people for works of service, so that the body of Christ may be built up"? (Eph. 4:12) We must be sensitive to the dangers of launching programs solely with good intentions and "carnal energy." [5] But we must also plan carefully, trusting that the Holy Spirit will lead.

BUILDING A COUNSELING MINISTRY

It is possible to wait patiently until problems appear and then to give whatever counseling help seems to be needed. The previous chapters have argued, however, that our helping ministries can be more influential and more effective if we actively reach out to people in need and sometimes intervene even before problems arise. How do we do this? Where do we reach?

To answer this, it is helpful to carefully and prayerfully seek answers to several crucial questions.[6]

Who Are We Trying to Reach?

Peter was called to bring the gospel to the Jews. Paul was intent on reaching the Gentiles. The apostle Thomas, according to tradition, was led to bring the Good News to India.

Far different has been the work of an unsung hero named Bill Eisenhuth, founder of a small nonprofit group known as Philadelphia Advocates for the Mentally Disabled. Every day, Eisenhuth works in a crisis intervention center. After hours, especially during the harsh winter months, he spends three to six nights every week bringing coffee, sandwiches, and encouragement to street people like Crawford.

In terms of your location, gifts, resources, and community needs, who should you be trying to reach? Your answer will probably include individuals and families within the church, but who are the unreached needy people in your neighborhood? It is right to give special attention to those "who belong to the family of believers," but the Bible also instructs us to find opportunities for doing good "to all people."

Are there lonely widows in your community? Are there teenagers hooked on drugs, frustrated parents, successful business people whose lives are empty, families with chronically ill relatives, housebound elderly people, the unemployed, new residents who are alone in your community, pressured single-parent families? Remember that you can't help everybody, but who *will* you reach?

What Are the Needs and Wants of These People?

It has been suggested that every well-designed, effective organization or system meets the needs and wants of the people whom it is trying to reach. A good hospital meets the health needs and wants of the community. A good school meets the educational needs and wants of the students, their parents, and the larger society. A good business meets the expectations of its customers.

An organization isn't likely to be successful if it has inaccurate information about people, or if it ignores what people want and need. Such an organization is in danger of producing products or services that nobody wants.

Some churches and counseling centers are like this. They have not followed Paul's example in Athens. The apostle had taken the time to understand the people. He knew that they were very religious idol worshipers, who had a number of objects for worship, including an "unknown god." Paul had learned that the men in Athens were debaters, and he knew that they were interested in "talking about and listening to the latest ideas" (Acts 17:21). Because he knew the needs, wants, and ways of thinking in his audience, he was able to help them more effectively.

It is easy to assume that we know what people need or want, but our perceptions may be partially or completely wrong. It is important, therefore, to listen to our intended counselees, to watch them, and to spend time learning about them. At times, you may want to get information about a group by distributing a short questionnaire, but think carefully about what you want to ask. Before you distribute the questions, make sure that they are clearly stated and understandable by the people you are trying to reach.

Many counseling ministries are ineffective because counselors haven't made the effort to understand what the counselee population is like and what the people want or need.

What Is Our Mission Statement?

In one of my counseling courses, I ask students to write a two or three sentence summary of their personal goals as counselors. This is not easy, but counselors can be more effective when they have thought through their goals and have clear direction for their helping ministries.

In designing a counseling institute, I once wrote the following mission statement. It may be too long, but it was intended to state our purpose in a clear, concise manner:

> The Institute exists to provide comprehensive, high quality, psychological services which include counseling, consultation, training, the dissemination of information, and opportunities for both study and research—all of which are based on assumptions, values and ethical standards that are consistent with biblical teaching. Our emphasis is on integrating psychological knowledge with biblically-based theology. Our goal is to have a local and world-wide outreach characterized by the most stringent ethical standards and the most reasonable costs possible.

What Are Our Goals?

Goals are more specific than a general mission statement. The best goals are clear, concise, realistic, and worth attaining.

In the counseling institute mentioned above, we wanted to focus on training. Our goals were set forth as follows:

Training sessions will be conducted both at the Institute headquarters and at other locations, under Institute sponsorship. Such training will be evaluated systematically by questionnaires and will involve (but not be limited to) the following:

- short (two-three hours) seminars;
- one-day seminars;
- one-week, two-week, and possibly one-month "in-depth" seminars; and
- the development of a speaker's bureau that would make speakers available for addresses and workshops at retreats and conferences.

At times, it is not possible to establish ministry or counseling goals that are this precise. Even when objectives can be clearly stated, the Christian must hold goals lightly and be willing to change direction if it appears that such change is a leading from God.

Please don't assume, however, that goal setting is only a luxury. When we know where we are going and what we are trying to accomplish, we often are more efficient and can help people more effectively. There is some value in the clichés: "Aim at nothing and you'll hit it." "When little is planned, little is accomplished." "The reason so many individuals (and churches) fail to achieve their goals in life is that they never really set them in the first place." [7] Can you list some precise goals for your people-helping work?

What Specific Programs Can Be Designed to Reach Our Goals?

In any organization, including the church, it is possible to be so committed to programs that we lose sight of people. From this, it does not follow that we scrap the programs.

Instead, we must design programs that are sensitive to the needs of people and that help us all move toward common goals.

In their book *People in Systems,* Gerard Egan and Michael A. Cowan state that programs are the means by which we reach goals. The best programs

- move step by step toward each goal,
- involve specific steps which are neither too complicated nor too difficult, and
- show a clear and logical progression from one step to the next.

Early one morning, I received a phone call asking if I would be program chairman for a large Congress on the Family. The previous chairman had left his position, and there was an immediate need for someone who could contact speakers and arrange both plenary sessions and small seminars for the two thousand participants who were expected to attend the conference.

Within hours, I was enmeshed in details of topic selection, schedules, speaker personalities, publication rights for papers, and a myriad of other details. It quickly became apparent that conference programs don't fall neatly into place. They take hours of careful planning and painstaking organization. Without priority charts, deadlines, and step-by-step procedures to help us reach our objectives, we never would have produced the conference program on schedule and never would have had speakers in their places at the designated times.

My experiences with that conference also showed the need for working together with others. Almost every successful program involves people who have the knowledge, skills, dedication, and persistence to carry out responsibilities as they move cooperatively toward common goals. Sometimes plans and programs come to a grinding halt because there are not enough people who share these characteristics. Effective people-helping programs, for example, need sensitive counselors with at least minimal training and a place to do their work. There may also be a need for funding, public relations within the church or community, and clear lines of responsibility.

Does all of this sound complicated? Have we lost our earlier focus on the church as a healing community? Have we slipped into a subtle professionalism and forgotten that all Christians should be what one pastor has called *stretcher bearers*—men and women who lift, encourage, and sometimes carry hurting people? [8]

For centuries, believers have been burden bearers (Gal. 6:2) even when they have no training in counseling and attend churches that have no formal counseling programs and ministries. Pastors have done pastoral counseling since the time of Christ, long before the modern pastoral counseling movement was born. These informal ways of helping are certain to continue.

But many laypeople and their pastors have discovered that demands for counseling are expanding rapidly. In our stress-saturated society, there is a great need for practical guidance to help people deal with personal, spiritual, family, physical, and other problems. Overworked pastors often cannot meet all the needs. Is a church-sponsored counseling center one way to deal with these demands?

BUILDING A COUNSELING CENTER

For some people, the words *counseling center* imply something threatening—a place where disturbed individuals go to get professional help in times of intense stress. Many counseling centers focus solely on one-to-one counseling within an office. They rarely employ the less traditional approaches that we have considered in preceding chapters. It is possible, however, to build a church-sponsored counseling center that reaches a variety of people and uses a broad range of helping approaches.

The director of a pastoral counseling center in Iowa has suggested that all organizations go through a life cycle. [9] Counseling centers, for example, often pass through a planning phase, followed by development, maintenance, and cessation stages. Each of these, including the last, can involve time and effort.

In the *planning phase*, the center organizers determine what needs exist. Who would the center reach? How would it meet local counseling needs? Where would the center be located? Who would work in the center? How would it be financed, used, or advertised? Questions like these must be prayerfully considered and carefully answered before a center is developed.

The *stage of development* involves creating and launching the center. The operation is likely to run more effectively if there is a clear statement of goals, precise job descriptions for center personnel, and an administrative structure that indicates who is ultimately responsible—especially when the counselors encounter a crisis.

The *maintenance phase* concerns the day-to-day functioning of the center. How can the center keep alert to changing needs in the community and congregation? Can it keep financially solvent? How can the effectiveness of the center be evaluated accurately? If these questions are not answered, the center may move to the final stage, *cessation,* where it ceases to exist.

Many churches attempt to solve these problems by hiring a trained counselor who is given freedom to work part-time or full-time in the church facilities. Such an arrangement can work well, but there still must be answers to questions about ultimate responsibility, payment of fees, confidentiality, or the relationship of the counselor to the church staff.

I have a friend who has counseled for several years in church settings. He has discovered the following several issues that need to be considered carefully when private counselors or counseling centers are sponsored by a church.

Organization and Purpose

Will your counselor or center focus solely on face-to-face counseling, or will there be preventive, public, lay, environmental, and other kinds of helping outreach? To whom will the counselors report in the church? Who will make appointments and what services will be offered? Will the pastor counsel in the center? Who will have access to the records? When such questions are not answered, there is potential for misunderstanding and frustration.

Some thought should be given to the counselor's location.

173

If his or her office is near the door of the church, some people will not come lest they be seen entering or leaving. To avoid this, counselors sometimes work in a house or other facility away from the church building. This helps to maintain confidentiality but adds rental costs.

Wherever the counseling takes place, it is important to have soundproofed rooms so passersby cannot overhear what is being said. Be certain, too, that the room is safe from intrusions. There are many stories of counseling sessions that have been interrupted because a deacon or Sunday school teacher innocently wandered into a church room where intimate counseling issues were being discussed.

Personnel

Who will work in your center? Will it be staffed by people who are poorly trained and not really qualified to counsel? In contrast, do you want to limit your staff to people with advanced degrees who expect to be paid professional-level salaries?

As a general rule, try to select counselors who are as competent and well-trained as possible. In a Christian counseling center, it is important to appoint people who have a deep commitment to Jesus Christ and who do not leave their Christianity at the door when they enter the counseling room. Professional counselors within the congregation may be able to suggest the names of prospective staff members, or you may want to get a recommendation from a graduate school or a seminary counseling faculty.

Many centers also seek the services of an outside consultant who can give guidance, suggestions, help in times of crises, supervision of counselors, and other professional help, especially when the counseling center is in its early stages of development. Unless the consultant is a church member, he or she will expect to be paid a consultation fee, but the price is likely to be well worth the services and protection that a consultant can provide.[10]

As you consider staff, don't forget to select receptionists and other clerical workers who can keep confidences and deal effectively and compassionately with counselees who might be distraught when they contact the center. Often, these important staff members are the first people to be in contact with counselees when they call the center.

Legal Issues

Depending on where you live, it may not be legal to establish a counseling center, even within a church. An increasing number of laws determine who is legally qualified to advertise, provide, and accept fees for counseling services. In most places, clergy are given the privilege of keeping information confidential if it is shared in a counseling session, but this does not extend to non-professionals. Some of the staff members in your center could be required to testify about their counseling experiences in a court of law.

Earlier, we mentioned a pastor in California who was sued by the parents of a young man who committed suicide. The suit charged that the pastor had prevented the man from finding the psychiatric help that might have prevented his untimely death. Would your center be protected against such litigation? What insurance do you need in order to pay court costs and penalties should legal action ever be brought against one of your counselors?

These are legal issues that vary from place to place and cannot be discussed adequately within a few paragraphs of a book. Before you establish a counseling center, please consult with a lawyer on matters of incorporation, licensing of the center and its personnel, confidentiality, tax-exempt status, insurance, protection from litigation, and other legal issues.[11]

Finances

Calcutta's Mother Teresa was once asked how she financed her work. "Money—I don't think about it," she replied. "It always comes. The Lord sends it. We do his work. He provides the means. If he does not give us the means that shows he does not want the work, so why worry?"[12]

Perhaps such a freeing and seemingly impractical viewpoint should be at the bases of all our ministries. It is important, however, to "count the cost" before we launch new ministries that might be expensive and a drain on other resources. Most churches have members with business expertise that can be of great help when the financial aspects of a counseling center are being discussed.

Will fees be charged in your center? If so, how much will be charged and does this have bearing on your tax-exempt status? Will the church members be charged as well as non-members? Will people of low income be charged the same as those who are more affluent? Will you seek donations to help the center? How will you pay for consultants, staff remuneration, insurance, soundproofing, and office expenses? For a small center, these may be minor issues, but each is worth considering before your center begins to operate.[13]

Center Philosophy

In the preceding pages, we have said little about Christian theories of counseling. As most pastors know, however, there is both controversy and debate about the best and "most biblical" ways to counsel.

Are all personal problems the result of the counselee's sin? Can the pastor really help a nonbeliever who has no interest in spiritual issues? Is there only one theologically correct way to counsel? Should Christian counselors reject, select from, or build on the theories of psychoanalysis, transactional analysis, reality therapy, rational-emotive therapy, or the work of Carl Rogers? What is the counseling approach that will be used in your center? When will you make referrals? Are there times when you will refer a counselee to someone who is not a believer?

These kinds of questions need to be considered before you select staff or announce the availability of your services. If you don't raise these issues, it is likely that somebody else will—sooner or later.[14]

DO YOUR HELPING EFFORTS REALLY HELP ANYBODY?

Psychologist Bernie Zilbergeld was not the first to question the effectiveness of his profession. For years, writers and speakers have been charging that counseling isn't nearly as effective as its advocates claim. Some of these criticisms have come from nontherapists, whose conclusions appear to be built more on prejudice than on fact. But this is not true of Zilbergeld. He is an experienced, well-trained therapist who carefully reviewed hundreds of research studies and concluded that counseling often is of no help, and sometimes even makes people worse.[15]

Are Dr. Zilbergeld's conclusions correct? A lot of debate still surrounds this question. Some counselors have presented case histories and testimonies to show how people have improved as a result of counseling. But such evidence is not very conclusive. Every counselor (Christians included) has at least some successes and is able to find counselees who can testify that they have changed. Instead of accepting these subjective reports, many psychologists and psychiatrists have looked beyond personal case histories and preferred, instead, to study the effectiveness of counseling by using rigorous scientific methods.

For some, the purpose of this counseling-effectiveness research is to find support for theories or to answer the questions of academicians. These can be worthwhile goals, but most of us are concerned with more practical matters. What are we doing that is effective and what is not effective? How can we change our approaches to make them more helpful? How can counselors best be selected and trained? Are some people more likely than others to profit from traditional counseling? Who is best helped by innovative approaches to helping? If secular approaches to counseling don't work well, is there any evidence from carefully conducted research to show that Christian approaches are better?

Since the time of Jesus, Christians have believed that the gospel changes lives, even though few, if any, rigorous scientific studies have attempted to prove the transforming power of Christ. Believers cannot judge success solely in terms of the world's standards or only with the aid of human measurement techniques. There is value, however, in carefully examining our Christian people-helping work in an effort to test its effectiveness and make it better. Our studies should be no less rigorous than the secular researchers who examine their own approaches so precisely.

Research Methods

Good research is time-consuming and often more difficult than you might realize. Assume, for example, that you want to know if counselees get better as a result of your counseling. How will you find out if this is true? You might have to start by defining what you mean by "get better." Can this be measured? How will you show that improvement is the result of your counseling and not due solely to the passage of time? [16]

Even if answers to these difficult questions are found, some counselors are threatened by research. How would you react if scientific studies showed that your counseling wasn't as helpful as you had hoped? Some people might think it is better not to do research so they won't have to risk facing the ego-bruising, painful possibility that their counseling isn't doing much good.

More often, I suspect, the lack of counseling research is not because we feel threatened but because we lack the time, energy, money, and expertise to do competent evaluative work. Returning to an earlier example, when people are drowning and need to be rescued, isn't it better to get on with the job of pulling individuals from the waters, instead of spending precious time and resources testing the efficacy of different life-saving devices? There might be value in hiring an outside research team that could measure our counseling effectiveness, but few counselors or counseling centers have the funds or desire to afford such a luxury.

In spite of all these difficulties, useful research can be done. A number of scientific techniques could be used to evaluate counseling effectiveness,[17] but one of the simplist is the use of a questionnaire.

Researcher James F. Engel suggests that such research should never be undertaken without a careful analysis of what you want to find. Do the church leaders or counseling center staff members really want to evaluate their effectiveness, and are they willing to make changes if the research suggests that things should be done differently? [18]

If you consider these questions and still plan to proceed with the research, a next step is to give careful consideration to what you want to discover. What questions would you like to have answered by your questionnaire? Who will take the questionnaire? When will it be given? When you have collected the completed questionnaires, how will you tabulate the data and what will the tabulations reveal that you don't already know?

Designing a good questionnaire is the next challenge. Try to keep your surveys short (twenty questions is a good number), easy for people to complete, easy for you to score, and limited to the important questions that you really want answered. Write and rewrite the questions before you give the survey. As we noted earlier in the chapter, it can be helpful to show the questions to several (three or four) people who are representative of the group that will complete the questionnaire later. Ask these few people to tell you what they think the questions mean (their answers might be surprising) and make revisions if needed.

When you are ready to take your survey, distribute enough questionnaires to get responses from a large percentage of the people whose answers you want to study. Remember that many will throw away your questionnaire and not return it. Can you be sure that the questionnaires that do come back are giving an accurate picture of what people think?

Research Reflections

If you have never attempted to do research, perhaps you can see why evaluations of your counseling and other work can be challenging but often difficult. Research can be worthwhile, but it is no panacea.[19] It can provide useful information, but what you do with the findings of your study will depend on your personal reaction to the results, your creative intuition, and leading from the Holy Spirit.

Psychology professors at local colleges may be able to give guidance if you decide to do more in-depth research. They

179

can advise you about research design, the importance of control groups, techniques to measure change, and ways that can help you avoid bias. They might also ask you to consider whether the research is worth the effort and whether or not doing your investigation will interfere with ongoing counseling ministries.

It might be argued that formal research is not needed if we want to reach and help needy people like Crawford, who walked the streets by himself for so many months. But it is helpful to know, accurately, who we are trying to help and what these potential counselees need. With everything considered, we are likely to find that prior planning and careful evaluation will enable each of us to become better people-helpers. This should improve the overall effectiveness of our counseling and caring ministries.

CHAPTER TEN

FUTURE COUNSELING

IT ISN'T a big or impressive building. There is no convenient parking lot (visitors have to find a place on the street), no massive entrance, no attention-grabbing sign, and no outward indication of the dynamic program that emanates from this plain building on Division Street in Chicago.

"We all experience pain at one time or another, need a friend, a shoulder on which to cry, a listening ear," wrote H. Millicent Lindo, the executive director of the Westside Holistic Counseling Center. "We respond with loving service to the needs of those entering our doors." The center "not only comforts the wounded spirit, but strengthens, encourages, and motivates" individuals to make "a positive contribution to family, neighborhood and society." The words of Psalm 90:17 are a constant reminder to the volunteer and paid professional staff workers: "May the favor of the Lord our God rest upon us; establish the work of our hands for us—yes, establish the work of our hands."

That work includes counseling with inner-city families and individuals; conducting workshops for pastors, teachers, parents, and others; running a day-care center for children; teaching parenting skills, especially to young adults; providing a variety of counseling services at neighborhood public elementary schools; maintaining an adult education program that helps participants earn a high-school equivalency diploma; giving classes in home nursing, single parenting, nutrition, and career planning; offering "Project OPT"—Options for Pregnant Teens—and "Project MANhood," a program to teach young males how to be responsible men; and tutoring adults who have never learned to read or write. The Westside Center may be simple in appearance, but its powerful, community-based programs reach far beyond the walls of its counseling offices.

Is this a model for the future of Christian counseling? Perhaps.

Each community is unique and no one counseling program, no matter how good, is likely to fit with ease into some other locality. There may be hundreds of community counseling centers scattered throughout the country and around the world. Each has been created by concerned people, often Christian people, who see needs in their communities and are reaching out to provide help. Most of the centers, like the Westside Center, operate with limited budgets but many trust that "the favor of the Lord our God [will] rest upon us" and "establish the work of our hands." [1]

EMERGING APPROACHES TO COUNSELING

One dictionary defines counseling as "the act or process of giving guidance to individuals." This is a broad definition. It includes, but is not limited to, the one-to-one sharing that takes place in a counseling room. The counselors at the Westside Center, at the clinic in Vellore, in the isolated communities of Alaska, in the villages near Mount St. Helen's, in that northern camp for inner-city teens, in the Philadelphia VA hospital where Crawford now lives, in emergency rooms all over the country, in military bases scattered worldwide, in your neighborhood and mine—all effective helpers must use a variety of approaches if people are to be cared for and needs are to be met. Compassionate counseling cannot be limited to one technique, confined to one location, or held within the boundaries of one rigid theory. Future approaches to people-helping surely will involve innovative, creative, flexible, diverse ways to help people solve problems, manage their lives, and change their communities. This is the essence of community psychology; it is the basis of true Christian care and counseling.

No one person can predict where this field of counseling will go in coming decades. Some have suggested that future counselors will be greatly involved in counseling the aged, working with nontraditional and increasingly unstable families, helping people handle leisure or cope with rapid change, working to prevent problems, and counseling with people who are more knowledgeable, more affluent, better educated, less industrious, and less religious than people today.[2] Some of the future trends are apparent even now and can be useful for counselors in the present.

Music, Art, Literature, and Poetry in Counseling

Will counseling in the future put more emphasis on some established tools from the past? When Saul was deeply troubled, David soothed the king with music played on a harp. Long before anyone had heard of art therapy, generations of people knew that doodling, painting, and other forms of creativity could relieve tension. Centuries before the current flood of self-help books, readers and advocates of "bibliotherapy" knew that comfort and guidance could come from reading the works of sensitive and helpful writers.

More recently, poetry has been described as "the latest word in healing." It probably is simplistic to assume that "whether a person is mildly depressed by everyday cares, or traumatized by rape or cancer, help is available through the poetry therapist" whose "dispensing of verses . . . may work better than Valium." [3] But the reading of poetry can be extremely therapeutic, and the writing of poems, as David discovered, can allow people to express their feelings and find relief.

Few would suggest that these ancient tools are, in themselves, all that we need for therapy. Nevertheless, these artistic modes of help may become more prominent now that people have more leisure time and are able to acquire music and books so easily.

Journal Keeping

For some people, few volumes are more therapeutic than the inexpensive notebooks that become personal journals. In chapter 3, we saw that a journal or diary is a place to record daily events, "a tool for self-discovery, an aid to concentration, a mirror for the soul, a place to generate and capture ideas, a safety valve for the emotions, a training ground for the writer, and a good friend and confidant." [4] John Wesley, George Whitefield, David Brainerd, Blaise Pascal, David Livingston, Thomas Merton, Francis Asbury, and a host of other spiritual giants discovered that journal keeping could be an aid to spiritual growth.

"For me writing is a very powerful way of concentrating and of clarifying for myself many thoughts and feelings," wrote Father Henri Nouwen in his thought-provoking and spiritually moving *Genesee Diary*. [5] Like generations before him, Nouwen has discovered how lives can be enriched when we write down our spiritual insights, our struggles, and our reflections on the Scriptures. Is it surprising that one secular writer has developed an entire approach to therapy based on the keeping of an "intensive journal"? [6]

This is a form of the homework mentioned in an earlier chapter. When counselees are encouraged to keep a journal, they continue to work on their problems between counseling sessions. Perhaps it should be mentioned that journal keeping can also be personally therapeutic for the counselor.

Audio and Video Recordings

Sermons and public lectures have been around for centuries; radio, television, phonograph records, audiocassettes, video recordings, and similar electronic devices are all relatively recent. The early leaders in the field of counseling never dreamed that their children would be part of a generation that could listen to self-help audiocassettes, get "media counseling" through radio and television, view films that teach interpersonal communication skills, and watch themselves on video tape.

As recently as 1973, *Time* magazine [7] reported on a new form of treatment known as "videotherapy." This term was criticized by some professionals, but the concept of using videos in counseling was accepted quickly. As video recording and play-back equipment has become less expensive, more counselors have been using video tapes to give instruction, modeling, guidance, and stimulation for discussions.

Videotapes of counselees can also be strong therapeutic tools. When counseling sessions are taped and played back, counselees can see, with glaring reality, how they are seen by others. Video feedback, it has been suggested, "enables the client to cut through layers of denial. When confronted with a picture [worth a thousand words] of one's behavior it becomes more difficult to deny that behavior." [8] After viewing such tapes, counselors and counselees can discuss specific behaviors and ways to bring change.

It is considered unethical to make audio or video recordings without a counselee's prior knowledge and consent; but, with the counselee's permission, is there any reason why such taping could not be used as a helpful tool in pastoral care and other forms of Christian counseling?

Audiocassettes have already proven to be extremely useful. Tapes can teach people how to relax, how to handle stress, how to study, and even how to counsel. In one widely used series, experts in counseling give taped guidance which counselees hear at home and later discuss with their own counselors.[9] In this way, the counselor's expertise and experience is supplemented by input from Christian professionals in the counseling field.

Computer Counseling

How would you like to go for counseling and discover that you would be talking, not to a warm empathic human being, but to a cold preprogrammed computer? Some research has shown that counselees are not as opposed to this as we might expect. In what has been called "high-tech therapy" by "compassionate computers," some counselees have revealed problems and insecurities about themselves that they have never been able to share with another human being. "I tried to tell you I was homosexual," one woman reported to her counselor after two years of therapy, "but I never could. It was less embarrassing to tell the computer." [10]

Experimental work has shown that computers can "listen" to counselees, analyze their statements, and make responses,[11] even though computers cannot show the warmth, sensitivity, understanding, and spiritual discernment that are essential for most counseling.

There are areas, however, where computers have been used with increasing effectiveness.[12] Consider the area of psychological testing. Only a few years ago, counselees would take psychological tests and then have to wait for several days, and sometimes weeks, before the tests could be hand-scored and the results interpreted. Now it is possible to have programmed test questions appear one at a time on the computer screen. After counselees type in their responses, the information is relayed by modem to a giant computer, and the results and test interpretations come back even before the test-taker leaves the office. Such testing is fast, efficient, often cost-effective, and liked by most counselees. The test results are then discussed with a counselor.[13]

Computers are also useful in vocational counseling. They can provide updated information about occupations and often can match test results with potential career choices. A number of reports have shown how computers also help people avoid potentially harmful job changes. One successful engineer, for example, was considering a move to management in his company. Computer testing showed that the man was an excellent engineer but would have made a very poor manager. He stayed in the work that he does best.

Computers have also been useful in helping people plan finances, control their time, reduce stress, and complete biofeedback programs that help resolve such problems as anxiety, tension headaches, hypertension, ulcers, and some types of asthma.

Sometimes counselees need information that a computer can provide efficiently. When the needed facts concern personal sexual questions or other potentially embarrassing topics, computers may be more helpful than human counselors. Probably, it is good that we have not yet reached the stage, predicted by one counselor, where couples enter computerized booths in shopping centers, answer a few questions, and get a computer analysis of their marriage strengths and weaknesses. It is frightening to think what might happen if the couple was left standing alone in a mall, reading a printout showing that their marriage was incompatible and deteriorating. This example, however, can give an awareness of the dangers as well as the potentials of future computer-assisted counseling.

At present, several tests are available that can be taken in the local church and computer scored for pastoral use.[14] More of these and other computer programs are certain to appear in the future.[15]

It should not be assumed that computer tests and other programs are more (or less) valuable than noncomputer counseling aids. Inaccurate and poorly designed tests can be given by a computer just as easily as they can be administered in paper-and-pencil form. Before choosing and using a test, ask who designed it, how the designer evaluated the test's effectiveness, and what evidence is available to show that the test measures what it claims to measure. This information is available to users of all valid tests. If the information is technical (as it often is) try to find someone to help you make sense of the psychological jargon. A psychologist or local guidance counselor can often give the clarification you need.

Physiological Issues in Counseling

Herbert Wagemaker is a psychiatrist in Kentucky who stumbled on an intriguing discovery. One of his colleagues was treating a schizophrenic who also had a kidney disorder. To the surprise of everyone, the dialysis that was given to treat the kidney problem also led to an unexpected improvement in the patient's emotional condition.

Could dialysis be used to treat severely psychotic individuals? Wagemaker's medical and psychiatric friends thought the idea was absurd, but the doctor persisted and began dialysis treatment with over sixty schizophrenic patients. Almost all patients improved dramatically. Apparently, the dialysis was removing a schizophrenia-causing compound from the bloodstream.

Further research in this area is continuing on both sides of the Atlantic. Experts are far from finding a physical cure for schizophrenia, but research like that of Herbert Wagemaker has shown that many of the problems we face in counseling may be at least partially caused by physiology.

Every counselor knows of people who fail to respond to months or even years of counseling and who improve dramatically when various forms of physical malfunctioning are discovered and treated. Premenstrual syndrome (PMS), for example, has received considerable media attention within recent years. Apparently, much of the depression, tension, and anxiety in women is related to biological aspects of the menstrual cycle.[16] Panic anxiety attacks in both men and women are now known to often have biological causes that can be treated medically.[17] One study (that coffee drinkers might like to ignore) found that high caffeine consumption increases both anxiety and depression in psychiatric patients.[18] There is truth in the old belief that tension drops when we drink less coffee.

Reports such as these should alert nonmedical counselors to the possibility that biological causes may be responsible for some of the symptoms that we may be treating as psychological or spiritual problems. No nonphysician can hope to keep abreast of all the research that deals with the physical implications of emotional disorders. That is the physician's responsibility, and counselors would be wise to suggest physical examinations, especially for counselees who are not getting better as the result of counseling.

Alternative Settings

Have you ever become so frustrated with existing schools, clinics, businesses, or counseling centers that you decided to start your own? Have you ever given up trying to get the government action on local problems and decided to take matters into your own hands? Do you know people who give hours of time and energy to establish day-care centers, nursing homes, Christian schools, suicide hotlines, alcoholism treatment programs, pregnancy-counseling centers, hot-meal programs for senior citizens, and other needed community services?

Throughout the course of history, literally thousands of individuals and community groups have taken responsibility for establishing "alternative settings" that are designed to bring services that are less bureaucratic and more effective, cost-efficient, available, compassionate, and morally decent than the helping resources that exist in the community. Many alternative efforts reflect dissatisfaction with current professional and governmental programs. Sometimes the spontaneous community projects begin with enthusiasm and fizzle shortly thereafter, but often there is a dedication and persistence that leads to creative and useful people-helping facilities.[19]

Alternative counseling centers or similar facilities are likely to continue making their appearance in the future. Before you refer people to any of these centers, it would be wise to visit the place where services are offered, to meet with the director and staff members, to inquire about the center's goals and philosophy, and to ask for all available literature. Who are the people who work in these centers? What are they attempting to accomplish? What is their attitude toward professional counselors? What are their religious beliefs? How do they respond to the church—including your church?

If you decide to establish an alternative facility of your own, expect that people will ask similar questions of you. Bathe every step of your planning in prayer and careful deliberation. A rereading of chapter 9 might help in your preparations, but don't neglect the advice of those "many advisors" (Prov. 24:6) who can give guidance and steer you away from potential problems.

Leisure and Legalities

It would be possible to continue for pages, and even for several more chapters, giving brief introductions to new counseling trends that are appearing. We have said nothing about the emerging field of consultation by professional counselors,[20] the new science of health psychology, the popularity of wellness clinics and holistic counseling approaches, emerging trends in the supervision and training of both lay and pastoral counselors, or the continuing growth of telephone counseling.

Then there is leisure counseling—an "emerging field" [21] that surely applies primarily to affluent Westerners who have the luxury of worrying over ways to avoid boredom and make use of their leisure time. When used effectively, leisure activities help people reduce stress, stimulate creativity, prepare for retirement, or restore balance to lives that have become too absorbed in work or other pursuits. Leisure counseling can be helpful, especially if we are able to find biblical perspectives on leisure. Perhaps someone will also develop a theology of leisure to guide Christian counselors.

Counselors must also be alert to emerging legal issues. These are no longer of concern only to lawyers or medical professionals. Within recent years, malpractice suits have become so common that even pastors have been sued for counseling malpractice. Many have been forced to take insurance against those who might bring legal action against church leaders.[22] In contrast to the past, counselors in the future will have to be more aware of the legal implications of their counseling work. If we ignore such issues, we risk facing financial and psychological pressures that could greatly interfere with our counseling ministries.

SERVANT APPROACHES TO COUNSELING

Randy was an exceptionally bright student. He was always at the top of his class, brilliant in his ability to critique counseling theories, a powerful speaker, and a clear writer. His fine mind was like an encyclopedia, filled with facts that could be tapped at will and brought to the surface instantaneously. He was an astute student of the Scriptures, familiar with the fine points of counseling methodology, and able to complete impressive scholarly research. His academic work indicated that he would make a very good counselor.

But there was one problem.

Randy couldn't get along with people. In spite of his outstanding intellectual abilities, he was insensitive, tactless, and often socially inappropriate. Reluctantly, but wisely, he abandoned plans for a career in counseling and moved to another profession where he was able to become successful in a field that required less contact with people.

Randy was able to recognize his area of weakness and move to a vocation where he built on his strengths. Maybe there are others who should do the same. Too many counselors— including pastoral counselors—appear to be intellectually capable but lacking competence in the area of interpersonal relationships. Too many training programs in seminaries and graduate schools have overemphasized the intellectual preparation of students but given little heed to the spiritual maturity, sensitivity, and interpersonal skills that are needed by anyone who wants to work with people.

Many years ago, Gordon Allport wrote that complaints "regarding the clergy generally have one principal basis—their alleged ineptness in handling human relationships." Are psychological counselors equally inept? Have we assumed that a knowledge of theory and technique is all that one needs for counseling effectiveness? Is it possible that I have written an entire book on helping skills and almost missed the most important ingredient in any type of helping: the helpers themselves?

In the hands of an inexperienced and insensitive physician, the most sophisticated medicine can be as dangerous as it is powerful. The same can be said of counseling knowledge. In the hands of an inexperienced and insensitive counselor, even the most effective and innovative counseling skills can be both powerful and potentially harmful.

Servant Counseling

Perhaps it never happened, but the story is told of a band of men who were on a journey to the east. They were accompanied by a servant named Leo who performed menial chores but also sustained the group with his uplifting spirit and constant singing. All went well until Leo disappeared, and the group fell into disarray. Without their servant, the travelers could not finish the journey so they abandoned the trip and returned home.

One of the travelers determined to look for Leo and spent several years of searching until the servant was found. To Leo's surprise, he was installed as head of the group that had sponsored the trip. He was proclaimed as the group's guiding spirit, its great and noble leader.

This story [23] stimulated Robert Greenleaf to conclude that great leaders are always servants first. In his thought-provoking book, *Servant Leadership,* Greenleaf developed the idea that the greatest leaders have a servant mentality. "This is my thesis," he wrote, "caring for persons, the more able and the less able serving each other, is the rock upon which a good society is built."[24] Like George Washington, who signed his letters, "Your most humble and obedient servant," truly great leaders have the desire and the capacity to serve.

Jesus taught this truth long before Leo got lost or George Washington started signing letters. When the mother of James and John asked that her sons be given prominence in the kingdom, Jesus replied that this was worldly thinking. It is not the same for believers, he said. "Instead, whoever wants to become great among you must be your servant, and whoever wants to be first must be your slave—just as the Son of Man did not come to be served, but to serve" (Matt. 20:26–28). Jesus was great because he was a servant.

Could the same be said for counselors? An up-to-date, working knowledge of theories, research conclusions, techniques, innovations, interpersonal relations, and helping skills can all be important and helpful. In addition, the Christian counselor must be intimately familiar with Scripture and characterized by a disciplined devotional life. But the essence of effective counseling, like the basis of great leadership, is that helpers must have a servant mentality. Great counselors are always servants first.

Most of us have noticed the frequency with which biblical writers emphasize helping and caring. Have you also noticed how often caring and a servant mentality go together?

In Romans 12, for example, believers are instructed to be loving, hospitable, sharing with the needy, rejoicing with those who rejoice, weeping with those who mourn, forgiving without taking revenge, active in feeding the hungry, and building peaceful relationships. All this helping is to be done by people who offer themselves as living sacrifices, who are not conceited, and who are willing to associate "with people of low position." Such helpers are clearly servants.

The Galatians were instructed to "serve one another in love" (5:13). The Colossians were to clothe themselves with compassion, kindness, humility, gentleness and patience, even before they began the servant's work of bearing with one another and helping others experience forgiveness (Col. 3:12–16). The Thessalonians were to live obediently—that is, how servants live—in ways that would please God (4:1). Then they could "encourage the timid, help the weak, be patient with everyone. Make sure that nobody pays back wrong for wrong, but always try to be kind to each other and to everyone else" (1 Thess. 5:14–15).

Jesus lived as a servant, and he expects his followers to do the same. To do so is not only to serve the Lord; the servant of Jesus Christ must also serve the whole community of believers (Mark 10:43f.; 2 Cor. 4:5),[25] and reach out beyond to "all people" regardless of their beliefs (Gal. 6:10).

The servant counselor is not an unskilled laborer who is manipulated by counselees and used as a convenient doormat. The servant is knowledgeable, competent, and—like Leo— willing to do menial tasks but is actively involved in helping people by giving encouragement and guidance. The servant is not motivated primarily by a desire to advance his or her own career, to keep people in counseling whether they need it or not, to charge unreasonable fees, to acquire fame and acclaim as a people-helper, or to push for the acceptance of one's own theory or methods.

The servant, instead, is like the capable administrator of Abraham's household. When he was sent to find a wife for Isaac, the servant prayed for wisdom, trusted God to give him success, used his training and thinking abilities to make a decision, took what action he could, and praised God for the subsequent result (Gen. 24).

That may be an ancient approach rather than a modern means of people-helping, but it is the message with which we must end this book. The truly innovative counselor knows about developments in the field and constantly works to develop creative counseling skills. The truly sensitive counselor recognizes that all counselees are part of a system and must learn to get along within a community of fellow human beings. But most important, the truly effective Christian counselor thinks like a servant, ready and willing to "serve the Lord with gladness" wherever and whenever God leads.

APPENDIX

Selected Helpful Books and Training Programs
for Lay Counselor Training

Adams, Jay E. *Competent to Counsel.* Grand Rapids, Mich.: Baker
Book House, 1970. This is Adams's basic introduction to nou-
thetic counseling. A Competent to Counsel Training Kit, including tapes and manual, is available from the National Association
of Evangelicals, 450 Gundersen Drive, Wheaton, Ill. 60187.

Backus, William. *Telling the Truth to Troubled People: A Manual
for Christian Counselors.* Minneapolis: Bethany House, 1985.
The author is both a psychologist and a pastor.

Collins, Gary R. *How to Be a People Helper.* Ventura, Calif.: Regal,
1976. This is a widely used text on lay counseling for Christians.
Also available is the People-Helper Pak, a twelve-hour training
program with tapes and manuals. Contact Regal Books, 2300
Knoll Dr., Ventura, Calif. 93003.

Crabb, Lawrence J., Jr. *Effective Biblical Counseling: A Model for
Helping Caring Christians Become Capable Counselors.* Grand
Rapids, Mich.: Zondervan Publishing House, 1977. This book
is not a training program, but Dr. Crabb does conduct lay train-
ing through his Institute of Biblical Counseling, 200 Seminary
Drive, Winona Lake, Ind. 46590.

Egan, Gerard. *The Skilled Helper.* 3d ed. Monterey, Calif.: Brooks/
Cole, 1986. This book is written by a psychologist-priest, but
it has no unique Christian emphasis. Nevertheless, it is widely
used in churches to train Christians. Somewhat difficult to read
(but worth the effort), the book is accompanied by a training
manual that contains helpful exercises.

Haugk, Kenneth C. *Christian Caregiving: A Way of Life.* Minneapolis: Augsburg, 1984. This book is a practical, easy-to-read manual
on Christian caring. It is written by the founder of the Stephen
Series system of lay caring ministry. This system is used in many
churches. For information, write Stephen Ministries, 1325 Bo-
land, St. Louis, Mo. 63117.

Walters, Richard P. *The Amity Book: Exercises in Friendship Skills.*
Grand Rapids: Christian Helpers Inc., 1983. This material is

available from Christian Helpers Inc., P.O. Box 7443, Boulder, Colo. 80306.

Welter, Paul. *How to Help a Friend.* Wheaton, Ill.: Tyndale House, 1978. This is a very good "how to" book with a Christian perspective. It could be read by trainees and used as a text, but it is not accompanied by a training program.

Worthington, Everett L., Jr. *When Someone Asks for Help.* Downers Grove, Ill.: Inter-Varsity, 1982. This is another well-written "how to" book for Christians. Useful as a textbook, it is not accompanied by a training program.

Wright, H. Norman. *Training Christians to Counsel.* Santa Ana, Calif.: Christian Marriage Enrichment, 1977. The author has written a number of excellent books on counseling, all of which are available from Christian Marriage Enrichment, 1913 East 17th Street, Suite 118, Santa Ana, Calif. 92701. Wright's *Training Christians to Counsel: A Resource Curriculum Manual* is a complete training program with tapes, available from the above address.

NOTES

Chapter 1
Community Counseling

1. Dr. Prashantham was once one of my students. We have kept contact since his return to India, and I have been privileged to give lectures at the Vellore center. On one of my visits, I gave a talk on "new and innovative approaches to counseling." Later, one member of the audience discreetly approached Dr. Prashantham and asked what was so innovative about what I had said. "That may be new in America," the man reportedly said, "but we are doing all of these things already in India." It is humbling and encouraging to see a student who goes far beyond his professor to develop innovative and creative approaches of his own.

2. Carol Turkington, "Psychology in the Last Frontier," *APA Monitor* 14 (April 1983):1, 12.

3. For an excellent survey of moral treatment, see J. S. Bockoven, *Moral Treatment in American Psychiatry* (New York: Springer Publishing, 1963).

4. T. H. Gallaudet, "Report of the Chaplain—1842," *The Journal of Pastoral Care* 33 (June 1979):136–38.

5. This term is a quotation from the time, according to Richard Almond in his excellent volume, *The Healing Community: Dynamics of the Therapeutic Milieu* (New York: Aronson, Jason, 1974). I have relied heavily on Almond's book during this part of the chapter.

6. Ibid., 89.

7. "Outreach in counseling" is a concept developed in a book by Chris Hatcher et al., *Innovations in Counseling Psychology* (San Francisco: Jossey-Bass, 1977).

8. Lawrence J. Crabb, Jr., *Effective Biblical Counseling: A Model for Helping Caring Christians Become Capable Counselors* (Grand Rapids, Mich.: Zondervan Publishing House, 1977), 190.

9. The psychological literature tends to use the terms *community psychology* and *community counseling* interchangeably. Since this book emphasizes counseling, especially that which is done within Christian settings rather than strictly psychological settings, we will generally use the term *community counseling*. Occasionally, the term *community mental health* will also appear. As defined by Ber-

nard L. Bloom (*Community Mental Health: A General Introduction,* 2d ed. [Monterey, Calif.: Brooks/Cole Publishing, 1984], 3), community mental health "refers to all activities undertaken in the community in the name of mental health." For a discussion of community counseling, see Judith A. Lewis and Michael D. Lewis, *Community Counseling: A Human Services Approach* (New York: Wiley, John, and Sons, 1977).

10. This figure is adapted, with permission, from the seven-dimensional model presented by Hatcher et al., *Innovations in Counseling Psychology,* 21.

11. David Drum and Howard Figler, "Outreach in Counseling," in ibid., 27.

12. "The Community Spirit," *The Royal Bank Letter* 64 (January/February 1983).

13. Almond, *The Healing Community,* xxi.

14. Ibid.

15. O. H. Mowrer, *The Crisis in Psychiatry and Religion* (New York: Van Nostrand Reinhold, 1961), 60.

16. Ibid., 70.

17. For a discussion of the church as a healing community, see Leigh C. Bishop, "Healing in the Koinonia: Therapeutic Dynamics of Church Community," *Journal of Psychology and Theology* 13 (Spring 1985):12–20.

18. See, for example, Robert G. Anderson, "The Role of the Church in the Community-Based Care of the Chronically Mentally Disabled: Reclaiming an Historic Ministry," *Pastoral Psychology* 28 (Fall 1979):38–52; Rodger K. Bufford and Trudi Bratten Johnston, "The Church and Community Mental Health: Unrealized Potential," *Journal of Psychology and Theology* 10 (Winter 1982):355–62; Howard J. Clinebell, *The Mental Health Ministry of the Local Church* (Nashville: Abingdon Press, 1965); idem, ed., *Community Mental Health: The Role of the Church and Temple* (Nashville: Abingdon Press, 1970); and Granger E. Westberg and Edgar Draper, *Community Psychiatry and the Clergyman* (Springfield, Ill.: Charles C. Thomas, 1966).

19. John Naisbitt, *Megatrends: Ten New Directions Transforming Our Lives* (New York: Warner Books, 1982).

20. The field of health psychology has expanded rapidly within recent years. For an overview, see Robert J. Gatchel and Andrew Abum, *An Introduction to Health Psychology* (Reading, Mass.: Addison-Wesley Publishing, 1983).

21. In an article on trends in professional psychology, it has been

suggested that "there is an overwhelming need for professional psychologists to become involved in military services. . . . serious concern must be expressed for both the human needs of members of the armed forces and their families and the state of readiness of those human forces in the event of warfare." See Walter F. Batchelor, "Future and Nontraditional Issues for Professional Psychology: Brief Perspectives," *Professional Psychology* 13 (December 1982): 765–70.

Chapter 2
Public Counseling

1. Joseph Veroff, Richard A. Kulka, and Elizabeth Douvan, *Mental Health in America: Patterns of Help-Seeking from 1957 to 1976* (New York: Basic Books, 1981). Thirty-nine percent of the people surveyed reported that they sought counseling help from pastors. No other group, including professional counselors, was selected as frequently for counseling.

2. Edmund Holt Linn, *Preaching as Counseling: The Unique Method of Harry Emerson Fosdick* (Valley Forge, Pa.: Judson Press, 1966).

3. Howard J. Clinebell, Jr., *Mental Health Through Christian Community: The Local Church's Ministry of Growth and Healing* (Nashville: Abingdon Press, 1965), 77–78.

4. John R. W. Stott, *Between Two Worlds: The Art of Preaching in the Twentieth Century* (Grand Rapids, Mich.: William B. Eerdmans Publishing, 1982), 190–93.

5. This is the conclusion of Lloyd M. Perry and Charles M. Sell, *Speaking to Life's Problems* (Chicago: Moody Press, 1983), 24. See also Donald Capps, *Pastoral Counseling and Preaching: A Quest for an Integrated Ministry* (Philadelphia: Westminster, 1980).

6. In writing this paragraph, I have risked facing the ire of preachers and homiletics professors who will maintain that a psychologist-layman shouldn't dare to write about preaching. I write, however, as a psychologist who has heard probably thousands of sermons "from the other side of the pulpit," conducted numerous seminars myself, and attempted to study public speaking carefully. Just as the nonpsychologist can often be helpful to people in my profession, I would hope that my comments could stimulate thought among those who may be great homileticians and orators, but who, for the sake of us in the pews, could be more relevant.

7. There are numerous books on good communication. Two of the best—one dealing with writing, the other with speaking—are William Zinsser, *On Writing Well*, 3d ed. (New York: Harper and Row, 1985); and A. Duane Litfin, *Public Speaking: A Handbook for Christians* (Grand Rapids, Mich.: Baker Book House, 1981).

8. Stott, *Between Two Worlds*.

9. Ibid., 61. A similar idea is expressed by Harry Emerson Fosdick, *Living of These Days* (New York: Harper and Row, 1956). He writes that the sermon should be "a co-operative dialogue in which the congregation's objections, questions, doubts and confirmations are fairly stated and dealt with (97)."

10. D. A. Carson, *The Sermon on the Mount* (Grand Rapids, Mich.: Baker Book House, 1978), 119.

11. Several years ago, Muggeridge aroused a stormy controversy when he publicly stated his opinions about the monarchy. Details of this can be found in Ian Hunter, *Malcolm Muggeridge: A Life* (Nashville: Thomas Nelson Publishers, 1980).

12. Malcolm Muggeridge, *Christ and the Media* (Grand Rapids, Mich.: William B. Eerdmans Publishing, 1977), 15.

13. Ibid., 45.

14. At this point, I must mention a film series that I once made on the subject of stress. I made the series reluctantly and only after a number of promises were made about the quality and content of the films—promises that were never kept. I make no apologies for what I said in the series, but the resulting films continue to embarrass me because they were so poorly produced. There are many committed, talented, highly ethical Christian people working in the media but, as I discovered, there are others whose work is a blemish on the entire Christian community.

15. Jane D. Zimmerman, "Psychologists' Multiple Roles in Television Broadcasting," *Professional Psychology: Research and Practice* 14 (April 1983):256–69; Elizabeth A. Klonoff, "A Star is Born: Psychologists and the Media," ibid., (December 1983):847–54.

16. See "We're Turning to TV to Talk Out Our Problems," *USA Today*, May 2, 1983, 4D.

17. David Lester, *The Use of Alternative Modes for Communication in Psychotherapy: The Computer, the Book, the Telephone, the Television, the Tape Recorder* (Springfield, Ill.: Charles C. Thomas, 1977).

18. If you are serious about talk shows, you could find much helpful information in Richard Mincer and Deanne Mincer, *The Talk Show Book* (New York: Facts on File, 1982).

19. One report suggests that, at any one time, there are at least 200,000 book manuscripts in preparation. Publishers are swamped with articles and book proposals or manuscripts, most of which are not likely to get published. This is the conclusion of Robert E. Alberti, *Your Perfect Write* (San Louis Obispo, Calif.: Impact Publications, 1985.) The book is a "manual for self-help writers," written for psychologists, but helpful to any writer of self-help books.

20. There is a scrap of paper on my desk in front of me as I write this book. I look at it several times a day, and its words remind me to pray: "Lord, I ask that the Holy Spirit will write this book through me. Please make it interesting, practical, clear, life-changing, and, above all else, Christ honoring." No Christian writer can be really effective if he or she forgets that we are only servants—operators of word processors through which the Lord works. Our goal is to be sensitive to his leading and to be willing to have him work through the abilities, training, and insights that he has given us.

21. Many of these books are published by Writer's Digest Books, P. O. Box 42261, Cincinnati, Ohio 45242. Helpful books include: Jefferson D. Bates, *Writing with Precision* (Washington, D.C.: Acropolis Books, 1981); William Gentz, ed., *Writing to Inspire* (Cincinnati: Writers Digest Books, 1982); Ethel Herr, *An Introduction to Christian Writing* (Wheaton, Ill.: Tyndale House Publications, 1983); Chip Ricks and Marilyn Marsh, *How to Write for Christian Magazines* (Nashville: Broadman Press, 1985); and L. Perry Wilbur, *How to Write Articles that Sell* (New York: Wiley, John, and Sons, 1981). See also, the previously mentioned books by Zinsser, *On Writing Well*, and Alberti, *Your Perfect Write*.

Chapter 3
Mutual Aid and Self-Counseling

1. Russell H. Conwell, *Acres of Diamonds* (Old Tappan, N.J.: Fleming H. Revell, 1960), 10–11.

2. This example is taken from E. Mansell Pattison, *Pastor and Parish—A Systems Approach* (Phil.: Fortress Press, 1977), 5.

3. This example, and research to back it up, is reported by Gerard Egan and Michael A. Cowan, *People in Systems: A Model for Development in the Human-Service Professions and Education* (Monterey, Calif.: Brooks/Cole Publishing, 1979). I have drawn much on

this book for my discussion on systems and counseling.

4. This is known as systems therapy, an approach that has become more popular in recent years. The numerous books by Jay Haley, Virginia Satir, and Salvador Minuchin give good secular introductions to this field. For a concise overview from a Christian perspective, see John A. Larsen's chapter on family counseling in *Helping People Grow: Practical Approaches to Christian Counseling*, ed. Gary R. Collins (Ventura, Calif.: Vision House, 1980), 113–31.

5. This is the conclusion of Robert S. Weiss, "Relationship of Social Support and Psychological Well Being," in *The Modern Practice of Community Mental Health*, ed. Herbert C. Schulberg and Marie Killilea (San Francisco: Jossey-Bass, 1982). For further discussions of support systems, see Gerald Caplan, *Support Systems and Community Mental Health* (New York: Behavioral Publications, 1974); Gerald Caplan and Marie Killilea, eds., *Support Systems and Mutual Help: Multidisciplinary Explorations* (New York: Grune and Stratton, 1976); and Benjamin H. Gottlieb, ed., *Social Networks and Social Support* (Beverly Hills: Sage Publications, 1981).

6. Although it is not written from a psychological perspective, Edith Schaeffer's book, *What Is a Family?* (Old Tappan, N.J.: Fleming H. Revell, 1975), is a folksy and insightful discussion of family support.

7. David E. Biegel and Arthur J. Naparstek, "The Neighborhood and Family Services Project," in *Community Mental Health and Behavioral-Ecology*, ed. Abraham M. Jeger and Robert S. Slotnick (New York: Plenum Publishing, 1982), 310.

8. Clinebell, *Community Mental Health* (see chap. 1, n. 18), 46.

9. There have been several studies of SRO hotel residents. These are summarized by Stanley Lehmann, "The Social Ecology of Natural Supports," in Jeger and Slotnick, *Community Mental Health and Behavioral-Ecology*, 319–33.

10. David Turkat, "Social Networks: Theory and Practice," *Journal of Community Psychology* 8 (1980):99–109; and Phyllis Ashinger, "Using Social Networks in Counseling," *Journal of Counseling and Development* 63 (April 1985):519–21.

11. Manuel Barrera, Jr., "Social Support in the Adjustment of Pregnant Adolescents," in Gottlieb, *Social Networks and Social Support*, 69–96.

12. Ashinger, "Using Social Networks in Counseling." The networking technique described in the text is adapted from this article.

13. See R. Bissonette, "The Bartender as a Mental Health Gate-

keeper: A Role Analysis," *Community Mental Health Journal* 13 (1977):92–99.

14. The OCSC organization can be contacted at P.O. Box 10308, Denver, Colo. 80210.

15. Lawrence E. Hinkle, Jr., "The Effect of Exposure to Culture Change, Social Change, and Changes in Interpersonal Relationships on Health," in *Stressful Life Events*, ed. Barbara Snell Dohrenwend and Bruce P. Dohrenwend (New York: Wiley, John, and Sons, 1974), 9–44.

16. James Mann, "Behind the Explosion in Self-Help Groups," *U.S. News & World Report*, May 2, 1983, 33–35.

17. In this book, I have preferred to use the term *mutual-aid* to describe the groups that meet together, and have reserved the term *self-help* for approaches in which individuals work on problem solving by themselves—reading self-help books, listening to cassettes, or using similar approaches. Most who write in this area do not make such a distinction. They use the term *self-help* to cover both the groups and the individual approaches.

18. Naisbitt, *Megatrends* (see chap. 1, n. 19). In light of the earlier discussion in this chapter, it is interesting to note that networking is listed as another one of Naisbitt's trends.

19. Michael Gershon and Henry B. Biller, *The Other Helpers: Paraprofessionals and Nonprofessionals in Mental Health* (Lexington, Mass.: Lexington Books, 1977), and Matthew P. Dumont, "Self-Help Treatment Programs," in Caplan and Killilea, *Support Systems and Mutual Help*, 123–33.

20. Later, when the Oxford Group movement became political and changed its name to Moral Rearmament, Tournier and others withdrew. The theological roots of mutual-aid groups are discussed by John W. Drakeford, *People to People Therapy: Self-Help Groups: Roots, Principles, and Processes* (New York: Harper and Row, 1978).

21. O. H. Mowrer, "Peer Groups and Medication: The 'Best' Therapy for Professionals and Laymen Alike," *Psychotherapy: Theory, Research, and Practice* 8 (1981):44–54.

22. In-depth analyses of the Mutual-Aid movement can be found in several published sources including the following: Alfred H. Katz and Eugene I. Bender, eds., *The Strength in Us: Self-Help Groups in the Modern World*, (New York: New Viewpoints, 1976); Alan Gartner and Frank Riessman, *Self-Help in the Human Services* (San Francisco: Jossey-Bass, 1977); George H. Weber and Lucy M. Cohen, eds., *Beliefs and Self-Help* (New York: Human Sciences Press, 1982);

and Emil R. Rodolfa and Lynn Hungerford, "Self-Help Groups: A Referral Resource for Professional Therapists," *Professional Psychology* 13 (June 1982):345–53.

23. This program has been designed and studied extensively by Phyllis Silverman at Harvard. She has written several papers describing her work, two of which are included in Schulberg and Killilea, *The Modern Practice of Community Mental Health,* and Caplan and Killilea, *Support Systems and Mutual Help.*

24. Andrew M. Greeley, "Pop Psychology and the Gospel," *Theology Today* 33 (October 1976):224–31.

25. See Alice Glarden Brand, *Therapy in Writing* (Lexington, Mass.: Lexington Books, 1980) and Ira Progoff, *At a Journal Workshop* (New York: Dialogue House Library, 1975). The most practical book in this area, written from a Christian perspective, is Ronald Klug, *How to Keep a Spiritual Journal* (Nashville: Thomas Nelson Publishers, 1982).

26. Quoted by Alan D. Hass, "The Book and the Couch," *Bookviews* (February 1978), 7–10.

27. Ibid.

28. This is the suggestion of Gary Alan Fine, "The Dangers of Popular Psychology," *Human Behavior* (June 1976), 12, 13. See also Janet Barkas, "Therapy Between Pages," ibid. (March 1975); 64–67; and Jane E. Brody, "Self-help Books," *Chicago Tribune,* April 8, 1979.

29. Some of these questions are adapted from Gary R. Collins, "Saintly Snake Oil: Weighing Church Quackery," *Leadership* 6 (Spring 1985):30–35.

30. Gershon and Biller, *The Other Helpers.*

31. John Z. DeLorean, *DeLorean* (Grand Rapids, Mich.: Zondervan Publishing House, 1985).

Chapter 4
Lay Counseling

1. The seminary was not the one where I teach.

2. John M. Darley and C. Daniel Batson, "From Jerusalem to Jerico: A Study of Situational and Dispositional Variables in Helping Behavior," *Journal of Personality and Social Psychology* 27 (July 1973):100–108.

3. David S. Shapiro, "Mental Health Professionals' Hangups in

Training Mental Health Counselors," *Mental Hygiene* 54 (July 1970):364–69; and Joseph A. Durlak, "Myths Concerning the Non-professional Therapist," *Professional Psychology* 5 (August 1973):300–305.

4. See, for example, R. Carkhuff and L. B. Truax, "Lay Mental Health Counseling: The Effects of Lay Group Counseling," *Journal of Consulting Psychology* 29 (1965):426–31; Robert Carkuff, "Differential Functioning of Lay and Professional Helpers," *Journal of Counseling Psychology* 15 (1968):117–26; and John L. Shelton and Rita Madrazo-Peterson, "Treatment Outcome and Maintenance in Systematic Desensitization: Professional versus Paraprofessional Effectiveness," ibid. 25 (1978):331–35. One review that has been less enthusiastic about lay effectiveness is that of Averil E. Karlsruher, "The Nonprofessional as a Psychotherapeutic Agent: A Review of the Empirical Evidence Pertaining to His Effectiveness," *American Journal of Community Psychology* 2 (1974):61–77.

5. J. A. Durlak, "Comparative Effectiveness of Paraprofessional and Professional Helpers," *Psychological Bulletin* 86 (1979):80–92.

6. Horace C. Lukens, Jr., "Training Paraprofessional Christian Counselors: A Survey Conducted," *Journal of Psychology and Christianity* 2 (1983):51–61.

7. Portions of this chapter, including the present section, were published previously in a journal article. See Gary R. Collins, "Lay Counseling Within the Local Church," *Leadership* 1 (1980):78–86.

8. Crabb, *Effective Biblical Counseling* (see chap. 1, n. 8).

9. At least one report found that careful selection is less important than careful training. See Lorraine E. Hart and Glen D. King, "Selection versus Training in the Development of Paraprofessionals," *Journal of Counseling Psychology* 26 (1979):235–41.

10. Gershon and Biller, *The Other Helpers* (see chap. 3, n. 19), 173.

11. Geraldine L. Cerling, "Selection of Lay Counselors for a Church Counseling Center," *Journal of Psychology and Christianity* 2 (1983):67–72.

12. The 16 PF, available to psychologists, is one potentially helpful test.

13. Cerling, "Selection of Lay Counselors."

14. Lukens, "Training of Paraprofessional Christian Counselors," 61–66.

15. This concept is generally attributed to F. Riessman, who suggested it first in "The 'Helper' Therapy Principle," *Social Work* 10 (1965):26–32.

16. Dr. Tan's work is mostly reported in a variety of excellent but unpublished papers, several of which have been presented at professional conventions. Dr. Tan is preparing a book on lay counseling to appear later in the Resources for Christian Counseling series.

17. Some of this professional resistence is discussed in John Kalafat and Daniel R. Boroto, "The Paraprofessional Movement as a Paradigm Community Psychological Endeavor," *Journal of Community Psychology* 5 (1977):3–12; and Michael J. Austin, *Professionals and Paraprofessionals* (New York: Human Sciences Press, 1978).

Chapter 5
Preventive Counseling

1. This term is used by Egan and Cowan, *People in Systems* (see chap. 3, n. 3). The authors advocate more emphasis on "upstream helping."

2. Gerald Caplan, *Principles of Preventive Psychiatry* (New York: Basic Books, 1964). The quotation is from Robert H. Felix who wrote the forward to Caplan's book and who, at the time, was director of the National Institute of Mental Health.

3. For an early discussion of this, see C. A. Roberts, *Primary Prevention of Psychiatric Disorders* (Toronto: University of Toronto Press, 1967).

4. The three recipients mentioned in this section are suggested by Bloom, *Community Mental Health* (see chap. 1, n. 9).

5. Some of these high-risk programs are described in Richard H. Price et al., eds., *Prevention in Mental Health: Research, Policy, and Practice* (Beverly Hills: Sage Publications, 1980).

6. W. M. Bolman and J. C. Westman, "Prevention of Mental Disorder: An Overview of Current Programs," *American Journal of Psychiatry* 123 (1967):1058–68.

7. See, for example, Robert D. Felner et al., eds., *Preventive Psychology: Theory, Research and Practice* (New York: Pergamon Press, 1983).

8. P. E. Johnson, "The Church's Mission to Mental Health," *Journal of Religion and Health* 12 (1973):30–40.

9. Some of these are discussed in Jay M. Uomoto, "Preventive Intervention: A Convergence of the Church and Community Psychology," *CAPS Journal* 8 (1982):12–22.

10. Felner et al., *Preventive Psychology*.

11. Summarized in Kenneth Heller et al., *Psychology and Com-*

munity Change: Challenges for the Future, 2d ed. (Homewood, Ill.: Dorsey Press, 1984).

12. This term was suggested by Norman Cousins, *Healing Options* (New York: W. W. Norton and Co., 1981). I have discussed the psychological implications of illness in chapter 5 of Gary R. Collins, *The Magnificant Mind* (Waco, Tex.: Word Books, 1985).

13. Caplan, *Principles of Preventive Psychiatry.*

14. Bloom, *Community Mental Health,* has a concise and helpful chapter on mental health education.

15. Several years ago, I decided to teach a Sunday school class on "Anticipating and Coping with Mid-Life." The leaders in my church were skeptical about such a topic, concerned lest it have no biblical content, and convinced that few people would attend. At the appointed time, the room was filled with people, many of whom expressed both enthusiasm and disappointment that the class didn't continue beyond its scheduled four weeks.

16. Life skills are discussed in detail in Egan and Cowan, *People in Systems;* in idem, *Moving Into Adulthood* (Monterey, Calif.: Brooks/Cole, 1980); in Gary R. Collins, *Getting Started* (Old Tappan, N.J.: Fleming H. Revell, 1984); and in Stephen J. Danish, Nancy L. Galambos, and Idamarie Laquatra, "Life Development Intervention: Skill Training for Personal Competence," in Felner et al., *Preventative Psychology.*

17. See J. Rappaport, *Community Psychology: Values, Research, and Action* (New York: Holt, Rinehart and Winston, 1977). One text has an entire section entitled "Prevention as Community Enhancement." See Jeger and Slotnick, eds., *Community Mental Health and Behavioral-Ecology* (see chap. 3, n. 7). Within recent years, a host of books and journals have reported on community enhancement programs that are designed to prevent problems. For a concise discussion, see F. D. Perlmutter, ed., *Mental Health Promotion and Primary Prevention* (San Francisco: Jossey-Bass, 1982).

18. Clinebell, *Mental Health Through Christian Community* (see chap. 2, n. 3).

19. Ibid., 28, 29.

20. Ibid., 262–63. For another look at prevention and the church, see Glenn E. Whitlock, *Preventive Psychology and the Church* (Philadelphia: Westminster Press, 1973).

21. The material in this section is taken from Howard Vanderwell, "Family Visitation as Preventive Counseling" unpublished paper (pastor of the Bethel Christian Reformed Church, Lansing, Ill.).

22. Ibid.

23. E. Cumming and J. Cumming, *Closed Ranks: An Experiment in Mental Health Education* (Cambridge, Mass.: Harvard University Press, 1957).

Chapter 6
Environmental Counseling

1. This quotation, and the material used in the three examples that begin this chapter, are all adapted from three articles under the general title "Crisis," *APA Monitor* 11 (September/October 1980):15–17.

2. Peter Kuriloff, "Counselor as Psychoecologist," in Hatcher et al., *Innovations in Counseling Psychology* (see chap. 1, n. 7), 37–62.

3. Ecological counseling and ecological psychology have become more prominent in the psychological literature within recent years. Most books on community psychology discuss these, as do a number of professional papers. See, for example, Malcolm Weinstein and Mark Frankel, "Ecological and Psychological Approaches to Community Psychology," *American Journal of Community Psychology* 2 (1974):43–52; Michael D. Jones and Norman R. Stewart, "Helping the Environment Help the Client: A Sequenced Change Process," *The Personnel and Guidance Journal* 78 (1980):501–6; and Jeger and Slotnick, eds., *Community Mental Health and Behavioral-Ecology* (see chap. 3, n. 7).

4. This classification is suggested by Albert Mehrabian, *Public Places and Private Spaces: The Psychology of Work, Play, and Living Environments* (New York: Basic Books, 1976).

5. Bonnie Lake, "My Office My Self," *Passages* 10 (1979): 61–78.

6. Olivier Marc, *The Psychology of the House* (New York: Thames and Hudson, 1977).

7. These issues are discussed further in Joan Kron, *Home-Psych: The Social Psychology of Home and Decoration* (New York: Clarkson N. Potter Books, 1983).

8. O. Galle, W. Grove, and J. McPherson, "Population Density and Pathology: What are the Relations for Man?" *Science* 176 (1972):23–30.

9. Sally Ann Shumaker and Janet E. Reizenstein, "Environmental

Factors Affecting Inpatient Stress in Acute Care Hospitals," in *Environmental Stress*, ed. Gary W. Evans (Cambridge, Mass.: Harvard University Press, 1982), 179–223.

10. Many of these conclusions are summarized in Mehrabian, *Public Places and Private Spaces*, and Evans, ed., *Environmental Stress*. See also Rudolf H. Moos, *The Human Context: Environmental Determinants of Behavior* (New York: Wiley, John, and Sons, 1976); Paul M. Insel, ed., *Environmental Variables and the Prevention of Mental Illness* (Lexington, Mass.: Lexington Books, 1980); and Heller et al., *Psychology and Community Change* (see chap. 5, n. 11).

11. U.S. President's Commission on Mental Health, *Report to the President*, vol. 1 (Washington: USGPO, 1978), 9.

12. Ibid., 51.

13. C. Mills, *Medical Climatology: Climactic and Weather Influences in Health and Disease* (Baltimore: Charles C. Thomas, 1939).

14. J. Oliven, "Moonlight and Nervous Disorders: A Historical Study," *American Journal of Psychiatry* 99 (1943):579–84.

15. See Moos, *The Human Context*, 93–95.

16. Andrew Baum, Jerome E. Singer, and Carlene S. Baum, "Stress and the Environment," in Evans, *Environmental Stress*, 15–44.

17. C. B. Flynn, *Three Mile Island Telephone Survey: Preliminary Report on Procedures and Findings* (Washington: U.S. Nuclear Regulatory Commission, NUREG/CR-1093, 1979). See also P. S. Houts et al., "Health-Related Behavioral Impact of the Three Mile Island Nuclear Incident," Report submitted to the TMI Advisory Panel on Health Research Studies of the Pennsylvania Department of Health, part 1, April 8, 1980.

18. S. Cohen, "Aftereffects of Stress on Human Performance and Social Behavior: A Review of Research and Theory," *Psychological Bulletin* 87 (1980):578–604.

19. In pondering this passage, I was helped by F. F. Bruce, *The Book of the Acts* (Grand Rapids, Mich.: William B. Eerdmans Publishers, 1971).

20. This is the suggestion of Robert E. Webber, "Church Buildings: Shapes of Worship," *Christianity Today* 25 (August 7, 1981):18–20. Following the Webber article, four brief articles appear to give a Baptist, Christian Brethren, Presbyterian, and Methodist reaction to Webber's Episcopalian perspective.

21. William A. Clebsch and Charles R. Jaekle, *Pastoral Care in Historical Perspective* (Englewood Cliffs, N.J.: Prentice-Hall, 1964).

Chapter 7
Brief Counseling

1. This is the opinion of J. Marmor, "Short-term Dynamic Psychotherapy," *American Journal of Psychiatry* 136 (1979):149–55.

2. See chapter 3. The shift from institutional and professional care to greater reliance on self-help is listed as one of our ten most influential national trends according to Naisbitt, *Megatrends* (see chap. 1, n. 19).

3. This definition is adapted from an excellent book on this subject, Richard A. Wells, *Planned Short-term Treatment* (New York: Free Press, 1982), 2.

4. According to Simon H. Budman, ("Looking Toward the Future," in *Forms of Brief Therapy*, ed. Simon H. Budman [New York: Guilford, 1981], 461), "Most brief therapies have an upper limit of 25 sessions and an emphasis on brevity of treatment."

5. B. L. Bloom, "Focused Single-Session Therapy: Initial Development and Evaluation," in Budman, *Forms of Brief Therapy*, 167–216.

6. This evidence is summarized in Wells, *Planned Short-term Treatment*, 2, 15–23.

7. Reported by Marmor, "Short-term Dynamic Psychotherapy."

8. Some of the research that supports client satisfaction with one-session counseling is summarized in Bloom, *Community Mental Health* (see chap. 1, n. 9), 60–63.

9. Summarized in ibid., 63–91.

10. L. R. Wolberg, "Short-term Psychotherapy," in *Modern Psychoanalysis*, ed. J. Marmor (New York: Basic Books, 1968), 353.

11. The program is described in detail in Gerard Egan, *The Skilled Helper*, 3d ed., (Monterey, Calif.: Brooks/Cole, 1986).

12. These characteristics are discussed by J. N. Butcher and M. P. Koss, "Research on Brief and Crisis-Oriented Therapies," in *Handbook of Psychotherapy and Behavior Change*, ed. S. L. Garfield and A. E. Bergin, (New York: Wiley, John, and Sons, 1978), 725–67.

13. Ibid., see especially, 738–39.

14. William L. Gets et al., *Brief Counseling with Suicidal Persons* (Lexington, Mass.: Lexington Books, 1983).

15. For a clear and detailed discussion of emergency psychology, see Diana Sullivan Everstine and Louis Everstine, *People in Crisis: Strategic Therapeutic Interventions* (New York: Brunner, Mazel, 1983).

16. Wells, *Planned Short-term Treatment,* 84–103. The discussion in the following paragraphs is adapted from this excellent book.

17. F. H. Kanfer, "Self-management: Strategies and Tactics," in *Maximizing Treatment Gains: Transfer Enhancement in Psychotherapy,* ed. A. P. Goldstein and F. H. Kanfer (New York: Academic Press, 1979).

18. William Glasser, *Reality Therapy: A New Approach to Psychiatry* (New York: Harper and Row, 1965).

19. This is summarized by Bloom, "Focused Single-Session Therapy."

20. Lewis R. Wolberg, ed., *Short-Term Psychotherapy* (New York: Grune and Stratton, 1965), 138, emphasis added.

21. Bloom, "Focused Single-Session Therapy."

22. Much of the research on counseling is summarized in Garfield and Bergin eds., *Handbook of Psychotherapy and Behavior Change.* In one study, it was found that counseled people actually got worse than those who were left to cope without counseling. See J. Fischer, *The Effectiveness of Social Casework* (Springfield, Ill.: Charles C. Thomas, 1976.

23. C. P. Rosenbaum and J. F. Calhoun, "The Use of the Telephone Hotline in Crisis Intervention: A Review," *Journal of Community Psychology* 5 (1977):325–39.

24. In an earlier book, I discussed practical aspects for telephone counseling in the church. See Gary R. Collins, *How to Be a People Helper* (Ventura, Calif.: Vision House, 1976), 84–99.

25. This is the opinion of Gets et. al., *Brief Counseling with Suicidal Persons.* I have drawn from their book in writing this section.

26. For a discussion of suicide from a pastoral and psychological perspective, see Bill Blackburn, *What You Should Know About Suicide* (Waco, Tex.: Word Books, 1982).

27. Some of these distinctions are summarized by Bloom in a chapter titled "Crisis Intervention," in *Community Mental Health,* 107–8.

28. This is a summary of the approach proposed by C. P. Ewing, *Crisis Intervention as Psychotherapy* (New York: Oxford University Press, 1978).

Chapter 8
Cross-Cultural Counseling

1. Derald W. Sue, *Counseling the Culturally Different: Theory and Practice* (New York: Wiley, John, and Sons, 1981), 4.

2. This term refers to people who go to other countries with the goal of evangelism, but who get jobs and work to support themselves within the culture. The word comes from Paul who supported himself and his ministry by being a tentmaker (Acts 18:3).

3. David J. Hesselgrave, *Counseling Cross-Culturally* (Grand Rapids, Mich.: Baker Book House, 1984).

4. This is described in a very practical booklet, written to help visitors adjust to other cultures: Shepherd L. Witman, *Some Factors Influencing Communication Between Cultures* (Pittsburgh: Pittsburgh Council for International Visitors, 1981).

5. Ibid.

6. G. C. Wrenn, "The Culturally Encapsulated Counselor," *Harvard Educational Review* 32 (1962):444–49.

7. This is discussed clearly by Judith H. Katz, "The Sociopolitical Nature of Counseling," *The Counseling Psychologist* 13 (1985): 615–24.

8. Walter J. Lonner, "Issues in Testing and Assessment in Cross-Cultural Counseling," ibid., 599–614.

9. Adapted from Daniel P. Kelly, "Receptor Oriented Communication: An Approach to Evangelism and Church Planting Among the North American Indians" (Ph.D. diss., School of World Mission, Fuller Theological Seminary, 1982).

10. Elaine S. LeVine and Amado M. Padilla, *Crossing Cultures in Therapy: Pluralistic Counseling for the Hispanic* (Monterey, Calif.: Brooks/Cole, 1980).

11. See, for example, Witman, *Some Factors Influencing Communication Between Cultures;* Katz, "The Sociopolitical Nature of Counseling"; and Paul Pedersen, "The Field of Intercultural Counseling," in *Counseling Across Cultures,* ed. Paul Pedersen, Walter J. Lonner, and Juris G. Draguns (Honolulu: University Press of Hawaii, 1976), 17–41.

12. Kelly, "Receptor Oriented Communication."

13. Adeyemi I. Idowu, "Counseling Nigerian Students in United States Colleges and Universities," *Journal of Counseling and Development* 63 (April 1985):506–9; idem, "Myths and Superstitions in Traditional African Healing," *American Mental Health Counselors Association Journal* 7 (April 1985):78–86.

14. Laura Uba, "Meeting the Mental Health Needs of Asian Americans: Mainstream of Segregated Services," *Professional Psychology* 13 (1982):215–21.

15. John W. Rosado, Jr., "Important Psychocultural Factors in the Delivery of Mental Health Services to Lower-class Puerto Rican

Clients: A Review of Recent Studies," *Journal of Community Psychology* 8 (1980):215–26.

16. Frances Everett, Noble Proctor, and Betty Cartmell, "Providing Psychological Services to American Indian Children and Families," *Professional Psychology* 14 (1983):588–603.

17. Tim Stafford, *The Friendship Gap: Reaching Out Across Cultures* (Downers Grove, Ill.: Inter-Varsity Press, 1984). This is excellent reading for anyone who contemplates prolonged travel or work overseas.

18. Ibid., 25.

19. Katz, "The Sociopolitical Nature of Counseling," 615.

20. Research to support many of these conclusions is reported in chapter 3 of Sue, *Counseling the Culturally Different.*

21. These have been gleaned from a variety of sources, including some of my own experiences in working cross-culturally. In this section, I have drawn from Sue, *Counseling the Culturally Different;* Hesselgrave, *Counseling Cross-Culturally;* and Farah A. Ibrahim, "Cross-Cultural Counseling and Psychotherapy: An Existential-Psychological Approach," *International Journal for the Advancement of Counseling* 7 (1984):159–69; John M. Dillard, *Multicultural Counseling* (Chicago: Nelson-Hall, 1983); and Howard N. Higginbotham, *Third World Challenge to Psychiatry* (Honolulu: University of Hawaii Press, 1984).

22. Sue, *Counseling the Culturally Different,* 108.

23. Ibid.

24. Ibid., 107.

25. Lewin's theory was stated most succinctly in K. Lewin, *A Dynamic Theory of Personality* (New York: McGraw-Hill, 1935). The application of Lewin's work to cross-cultural counseling is seen in the work of Allen E. Ivey, "Counseling and Psychotherapy: Toward A New Perspective," in *Cross-cultural Counseling and Psychotherapy,* ed. Anthony J. Marsella and Paul B. Pedersen (New York: Pergamon Press, 1981), 279–311.

26. Erich Fromm, *The Sane Society* (New York: Rinehart, Roberts, Publishers, 1955).

27. For an in-depth discussion of cross-cultural counseling and stress, see Elsie M. J. Smith, "Ethnic Minorities: Life Stress, Social Support, and Mental Health Issues," *The Counseling Psychologist* 13 (1985):537–79).

28. Some of these issues are summarized by James Allan Peterson, *Counseling and Values* (Scranton, Pa.: International Textbook Company, 1970).

29. The list that follows is taken from a description of American Indians. See Joseph E. Trimble, "Value Differences Among American Indians: Concerns for the Concerned Counselor," in Pedersen, Lonner, and Draguns, *Counseling Across Cultures*, 65–81.

30. For a discussion of ethical issues in cross-cultural counseling, see Paul B. Pedersen and Anthony J. Marsella, "The Ethical Crisis for Cross-Cultural Counseling and Therapy," *Professional Psychology* 13 (1982):492–500.

Chapter 9
Planning Counseling

1. J. F. Kennedy, *Message from the President of the United States Relative to Mental Illness and Mental Retardation*, 88th Cong., 1st sess., House of Representatives Doc. 58. (Washington, D.C.: Government Printing Office, 1963).

2. Donald C. Drake, "The Forsaken: How America has Abandoned Troubled Thousands in the Name of Social Progress," *The Philadelphia Inquirer*, July 18–24, 1982. This was a series of articles based on eighteen months of investigative reporting by Drake who followed released mental patients who were barely able to cope.

3. The wisdom and importance of planning is discussed by Marshall Shelly, "What's a Body to Do?" *Leadership* 5 (Winter 1984): 38–43.

4. Jack W. Hayford, "Why I Don't Set Goals," *Leadership* 5 (Winter 1984):46–51. The quotation that follows is from p. 51, and used with permission.

5. Ibid., 50.

6. These questions have been developed primarily as a result of my reflections on two important books: Egan and Cowan, *People in Systems* (see chap. 3, n. 3), and Edwin J. Thomas, *Designing Interventions for the Helping Professions* (Beverly Hills: Sage Publications, 1984). I have used these questions successfully in planning several counseling projects, but their influence goes beyond the design of counseling ministries.

7. Denis Waitley, *Seeds of Greatness* (Old Tappan, N.J.: Fleming H. Revell, 1983), 101.

8. Michael Slater, *Stretcher Bearers* (Ventura, Calif.: Regal Books, 1985).

9. Richard E. Guest, "Community Resources and the Process of

Pastoral Counseling Center Development," in *The Organization and Administration of Pastoral Counseling Centers,* eds. John C. Carr, John E. Hinkle, and David M. Moss, III (Nashville: Abingdon, 1981), 39–56.

10. For further discussions of the selection and use of consultants, please see chapters 10 and 11 in ibid.

11. Richard E. Augspurger gives additional legal advice in chapter 8, "Legal Concerns of the Pastoral Counselor," in ibid., 131–48.

12. Quoted by Kathryn Spink, *Miracle of Love* (New York: Harper and Row, 1981).

13. Business, financial, and fee-setting matters are discussed in chapters 5, 6, and 7, Carr, Hinkle, and Moss, eds., *Organization and Administration, 130.*

14. Some Christian approaches to counseling have been summarized in a volume edited by the author of this book. See Collins, ed., *Helping People Grow* (see chap. 3, n. 4). Philosophical issues related to counseling centers are considered in several chapters of Carr, Hinkle, and Moss, *Organization and Administration.* See for example, the chapter by Emily Demme Haight, "Issues of Clinical Practice in Pastoral Counseling Centers," ibid., 150–64.

15. Bernie Zilbergeld, *The Shrinking of America: Myths of Psychological Change* (Boston: Little, Brown, 1983). An excerpt from Zilbergeld's book, followed by responses from four Christian counselors, appeared in *Leadership* 5 (Winter 1984):87–94.

16. There are numerous books and articles summarizing both the difficulties and the findings of research on the effectiveness of counseling and psychotherapy. One of the most complete summaries is by Sol L. Garfield and Allen E. Bergin, ed., *Handbook of Psychotherapy and Behavior Change: An Empirical Analysis,* 2d ed., (New York: Wiley, 1978). Evaluations of community psychology are found in Walter E. Barton and Charlotte J. Sanborn, eds., *An Assessment of the Community Mental Health Movement* (Lexington, Mass.: Lexington Books, 1977). For a more recent update, see Sol L. Garfield, "Effectiveness of Psychotherapy: The Perennial Controversy," *Professional Psychology* 14 (February 1983):35–43.

17. See Steven C. Nahrwold, John L. Florell, and David M. Moss, III, "Pastoral Counseling Centers and Evaluative Research," in Carr, Hinkle, and Moss, *Organization and Administration,* 256–88. A more complete discussion appears in a chapter by Emory L. Cowen and Ellis L. Gesten, "Evaluating Community Programs: Tough and Tender Perspectives," in *Community Psychology: Theoretical and Empirical Approaches,* ed. Margaret S. Gibbs, Juliana Rasic Lachen-

meyer, and Janet Sigal (New York: Gardner Press, 1980), 363–93.

18. James F. Engel, "Sidestepping Pitfalls in Congregational Research," *Leadership* 5 (Winter 1984):26–29.

19. Ibid., makes this point. For a booklet on basic research for congregations, see Engel, *How Can I Get Them to Listen?* available from Management Development Associates, 1403 N. Main, Suite 207, Wheaton, Ill. 60187.

Chapter 10
Future Counseling

1. More information on the creative programs at the Westside Holistic Family Center can be obtained by writing to the Center at 5437 West Division Street, Chicago, Ill. 60651.

2. These are some of the predictions of John M. Whiteley, "Counseling in the Year 2000 A.D.," *The Counseling Psychologist* 8 (1980):2–8. This entire issue of the journal is devoted to counseling trends. See also an entire issue of ibid., 10 (1982) devoted to "Counseling Psychology: The Next Decade."

3. Quoted by Jody Kolodzey in "Poetry: The Latest Word in Healing," *Prevention* (January 1983), 62–68.

4. Ronald Klug, *How to Keep a Spiritual Journal* (Nashville: Thomas Nelson Publishers, 1982), 9. Klug's book is a little-known but excellent practical guide to journal keeping.

5. Henri J. M. Nouwen, *The Genesee Diary: Report from a Trappist Monastery* (Garden City, N.Y.: Image Books, 1981), 121.

6. Ira Progoff, *At a Journal Workshop* (New York: Dialogue House Library, 1975).

7. V. Adams, "Videotherapy," *Time*, Feb. 26, 1973, 58.

8. Ira Heilveil, *Video in Mental Health Practice: An Activities Handbook* (New York: Springer Publishing, 1983), 4. Heilveil's book is an excellent and practical introduction to the use of video recordings in counseling. The book contains a very good bibliography.

9. Known as the Christian Counselor's Library, this series of twenty-eight cassette tapes, along with complete instructions for their use, is available from Word, Inc., 4800 West Waco Drive, Waco, Tex. 76796. The tape series and accompanying materials were designed by Gary R. Collins, the author of this book.

10. Reported in Jon Van, "High-Tech Therapy: The Compassionate Computer Finds a Home in Psychiatry," *Chicago Tribune*, May 29, 1983.

11. G. Brian Jones, Jo Ann Harris-Bowlsbey, and David V. Tiedman, "Computer Technology in Counseling," in Hatcher et al., *Innovations in Counseling Psychology* (see chap. 1, n. 7), 248–85.

12. See, for example, Dona Alpert, Charles J. Pulvino, and James L. Lee, "Computer Applications in Counseling: Some Practical Suggestions," *Journal of Counseling and Development* 63 (April 1985):522–23.

13. Bruce Duthie, "A Critical Examination of Computer Administered Tests," in *Using Computers in Clinical Practice: Psychotherapy and Mental Health Applications,* ed. Marc D. Schwartz (New York: Haworth Press, 1984), 135–39. The Schwartz book is an excellent collection of sixty chapters dealing with computer use in counseling. For additional information, see *The Counseling Psychologist* 11 (1983). This entire issue is devoted to "Computer Assisted Counseling."

14. The Taylor-Johnson Temperament Analysis (T-JTA), for example, can be computer scored and interpreted. For more information, contact Psychological Publications, Inc., 5300 Hollywood Boulevard, Los Angeles, Calif. 90027.

15. Some readers may want to obtain a small (thirty-eight-page) pamphlet, *Computers and the Church,* written by Mike Davis and Steve Clapp, and available from C-4 Resources, P. O. Box 1408, Champaign, Ill. 61820.

16. The local library can probably provide more information. See, for example, Elizabeth Gonzalez, "Premenstrual Syndrome: An Ancient Woe Deserving Modern Scrutiny," *Journal of the American Medical Association* 243 (April 10, 1981):1393–96.

17. David V. Scheehan, *The Anxiety Disease* (New York: Charles Schribner's Sons, 1983).

18. John F. Greden et al., "Anxiety and Depression Associated with Caffeinism Among Psychiatric Inpatients," *American Journal of Psychiatry* 135 (August 1978):963–66.

19. For further information on alternative settings, see Chris Hatcher, "Dreams and Realities of Alternative Counseling Centers," in Hatcher et al., *Innovations in Counseling Psychology,* 199–218; chap. 9, "Alternative Settings and Social Change," in Heller et al., *Psychology and Community Change* (see chap. 4, n. 11), 286–336; and E. L. Cowen, "Help is Where You Find It: Four Informal Helping Groups," *American Psychologist* 37 (1982):385–95.

20. June Gallessich, *The Profession and Practice of Consultation* (San Francisco: Jossey/Bass, 1982).

21. The term is used by E. Thomas Dowd, "Leisure Counseling:

Summary of an Emerging Field," *The Counseling Psychologist* 9 (1981):81–82. This entire issue is devoted to papers on leisure counseling.

22. For an insightful and sobering discussion of the malpractice issue, see Sara C. Charles and Eugene Kennedy, *Defendant: A Psychiatrist on Trial for Medical Malpractice* (New York: Free Press, 1985). Written like a novel (Kennedy is a successful novelist), this true account has relevance for all counselors.

23. Hermann Hesse, *Journey to the East* trans. Hilda Rosner (New York: Farrar, Straus and Giroux, 1956).

24. Robert K. Greenleaf, *Servant Leadership* (New York: Paulist Press, 1977), 49.

25. J. R. Michaels, "Servant," in *The Zondervan Pictoral Encyclopedia of the Bible,* ed. Merrill C. Tenney, vol. 5 (Grand Rapids, Mich.: Zondervan Publishing House, 1975), 358–60.

INDEX

Gary R. Collins

Gary R. Collins is a licensed psychologist with a Ph.D. in clinical psychology from Purdue University. He has published numerous scientific and popular articles, serves as consulting editor to two professional journals, and is a contributing editor to *Christian Herald*. His books include *How to be a People Helper, Christian Counseling,* and *The Magnificent Mind*. He is the General Editor for the Resources for Christian Counseling series, published by Word, Inc.

Until recently, Dr. Collins was chairman of the Division of Counseling and professor of psychology at Trinity Evangelical Divinity School. He still teaches half-time at Trinity, but is also involved in writing, speaking, and leading workshops, frequently overseas. He lives in northern Illinois with his wife Julie and two college age daughters, Marilynn and Jan.